Decorating with

ARCHITECTURAL
DETAILS

CRE**A**TIVE
HOMEOWNER®

Decorating with

ARCHITECTURAL
DETAILS

Philip Schmidt

Photography by
Jessie Walker

CREATIVE HOMEOWNER®, Upper Saddle River, New Jersey

VP / EDITORIAL DIRECTOR: Timothy O. Bakke
PRODUCTION MANAGER: Kimberly H. Vivas

SENIOR EDITOR: Fran J. Donegan
PHOTO EDITOR / ASSISTANT EDITOR: Jennifer Ramcke
EDITORIAL ASSISTANT: Jennifer Doolittle
COPY EDITOR: Ellen Ellender
INDEXER: Schroeder Indexing Services

ART DIRECTION / LAYOUT: David Geer
PHOTOGRAPHY: Jesse Walker
ILLUSTRATIONS: Robert LaPointe

Manufactured in the United States of America

Current Printing (last digit)
10 9 8 7 6 5 4 3 2 1

Decorating with Architectural Details
Library of Congress Catalog Card Number: 2003112861
ISBN: 1-58011-157-2

CREATIVE HOMEOWNER®
A Division of Federal Marketing Corp.
24 Park Way, Upper Saddle River, NJ 07458
www.creativehomeowner.com

METRIC EQUIVALENTS

All measurements in this book are given in U.S. Customary units. If you wish to find metric equivalents, use the following table and conversion factors.

LENGTH

1 inch	25.4 mm
1 foot	0.3048 m
1 yard	0.9144 m
1 mile	1.61 km

AREA

1 square inch	645 mm^2
1 square foot	0.0929 m^2
1 square yard	0.8361 m^2
1 acre	4046.86 m^2
1 square mile	2.59 km^2

VOLUME

1 cubic inch	16.3870 cm^3
1 cubic foot	0.03 m^3
1 cubic yard	0.77 m^3

CAPACITY

1 fluid ounce	29.57 ml
1 pint	473.18 ml
1 quart	1.14 l
1 gallon	3.79 l

WEIGHT

1 ounce	28.35g
1 pound	0.45kg

TEMPERATURE

Fahrenheit = Celsius × 1.8 + 32
Celsius = Fahrenheit - 32 × ⅝

NAIL SIZE & LENGTH

Penny Size	Nail Length
2d	1"
3d	1¼"
4d	1½"
5d	1¾"
6d	2"
7d	2¼"
8d	2½"
9d	2¾"
10d	3"
12d	3¼"
16d	3½"

SAFETY

Although the methods in this book have been reviewed for safety, it is not possible to overstate the importance of using the safest methods you can. What follows are reminders—some do's and don'ts of work safety—to use along with your common sense.

> Always use caution, care, and good judgment when following the procedures described in this book.

> Always be sure that the electrical setup is safe, that no circuit is overloaded, and that all power tools and outlets are properly grounded. Do not use power tools in wet locations.

> Always read container labels on paints, solvents, and other products; provide ventilation; and observe all other warnings.

> Always read the manufacturer's instructions for using a tool, especially the warnings.

> Use hold-downs and push sticks whenever possible when working on a table saw. Avoid working short pieces if you can.

> Always remove the key from any drill chuck (portable or press) before starting the drill.

> Always pay deliberate attention to how a tool works so that you can avoid being injured.

> Always know the limitations of your tools. Do not try to force them to do what they were not designed to do.

> Always make sure that any adjustment is locked before proceeding. For example, always check the rip fence on a table saw or the bevel adjustment on a portable saw before starting to work.

> Always clamp small pieces to a bench or other work surface when using a power tool.

> Always wear the appropriate rubber gloves or work gloves when handling chemicals, moving or stacking lumber, working with concrete, or doing heavy construction.

> Always wear a disposable face mask when you create dust by sawing or sanding. Use a special filtering respirator when working with toxic substances and solvents.

> Always wear eye protection, especially when using power tools or striking metal on metal or concrete; a chip can fly off, for example, when chiseling concrete.

> Never work while wearing loose clothing, open cuffs, or jewelry; tie back long hair.

> Always be aware that there is seldom enough time for your body's reflexes to save you from injury from a power tool in a dangerous situation; everything happens too fast. Be alert!

> Always keep your hands away from the business ends of blades, cutters, and bits.

> Always hold a circular saw firmly, usually with both hands.

> Always use a drill with an auxiliary handle to control the torque when using large-size bits.

> Always check your local building codes when planning new construction. The codes are intended to protect public safety and should be observed to the letter.

> Never work with power tools when you are tired or when under the influence of alcohol or drugs.

> Never cut tiny pieces of wood or pipe using a power saw. When you need a small piece, saw it from a securely clamped longer piece.

> Never change a saw blade or a drill or router bit unless the power cord is unplugged. Do not depend on the switch being off. You might accidentally hit it.

> Never work in insufficient lighting.

> Never work with dull tools. Have them sharpened, or learn how to sharpen them yourself.

> Never use a power tool on a workpiece—large or small—that is not firmly supported.

> Never saw a workpiece that spans a large distance between horses without close support on each side of the cut; the piece can bend, closing on and jamming the blade, causing saw kickback.

> When sawing, never support a workpiece from underneath with your leg or other part of your body.

> Never carry sharp or pointed tools, such as utility knives, awls, or chisels, in your pocket. If you want to carry any of these tools, use a special-purpose tool belt that has leather pockets and holders.

CONTENTS

INTRODUCTION

When architects of the past designed homes, they applied their art not only to the facade but also the interior spaces, filling the rooms with decorative ornament that created distinctive settings for everyday life. From the classical columns of wealthy colonists' homes to Victorian molding treatments to Craftsman-style built-ins, these architectural details were part of the original blueprints and were integral to the homes' interior designs. They were added with forethought given to the use and social importance of each room—just as good decorators do today. By contrast, efficiency of design and cost-effective building have left most modern homes bereft of all but the simplest architectural ornament; often baseboard trim and plain window and door casings are the only built-in decorations. These homes are full of opportunities for adding architectural character.

Covering dozens of traditional details and their uses, this book can help you decorate with timeless style and architectural relevance. Each chapter includes professional decorating tips for adding ornament, along with photographs that show details applied in a range of settings both contemporary and traditional. Through technical illustrations, planning advice, and simple how-to steps, you'll learn the essentials of installing store-bought details as well as designing and building your own projects. A reference chapter on tools, materials, and techniques covers the basics of building materials and guides you through some of the trickier jobs, like cutting crown molding and finishing drywall.

Thanks to the many well-designed products available, adding architectural details is well within the ability of most do-it-yourselfers. Millwork companies, architectural products dealers, and specialty manufacturers produce a complete range of details in modern and traditional materials. Some are authentic reproductions of historic designs, while other products, such as trimwork, are fun-

Thanks to the variety of architectural products, you can find the details that will enhance your home. Those shown here include a formal mantel, top, a Craftsman-style stair detail, above, and a classic pillar and entablature, left.

damental decorating tools that have been used by builders and designers for centuries. And for truly old details, there's a burgeoning nationwide market of architectural salvage—for those interested in the art of finding new uses for old things.

For inspiration, home decorators can look to Thomas Jefferson, America's greatest amateur architect and consummate do-it-yourselfer, who tinkered with his Monticello home for over five decades, always blending styles and details of the past with his own creative vision. Here's to the Jefferson in all of us.

Some details offer practical as well as ornamental uses. The decorative shelf that resembles a mantelshelf over the cooktop, above, hides the vent hood; window seats, right, often contain built-in storage areas under the cushions.

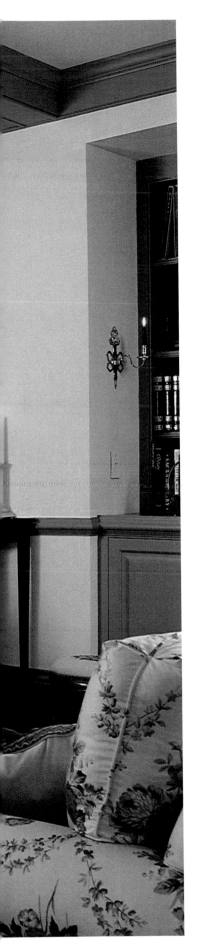

CHAPTER 1

ARCHITECTURAL DETAILS
IN HOME DESIGN

*A*rchitectural details are permanent features and fixtures that shape a home's interior landscape. Trimwork or molding usually has a practical application, such as hiding a seam between building materials. And while many architectural details, such as columns, window seats, built-in shelving, mantels, and trimmed wall openings, also serve practical functions, they are valued more for what they contribute to a room's design or ornamentation. They tend to play a larger more significant role in a home's interior design. Architectural details go beyond standard molding and trim. They can be a design focal point or, as is the case with ornate molding, work with other elements in the room to present a unified design theme.

Adding Architectural Details

Architectural details can improve your home in ways that standard decorating tools cannot. For example, while a couch provides a comfortable place to sit, a window seat connects a living area with the outdoors; whereas a change of carpeting signals a transition into a dining room, a passageway of stately columns creates a grand entrance.

DECORATING BASICS

When incorporating architectural details in your home, stay mindful of the basic decorating considerations of style, size, and balance. Most modern interiors are eclectic in style, often not by any conscious decorating effort but because a less rigid style suits the somewhat generic architecture of modern home design, as well as the modern lifestyle. Eclecticism allows for architectural details in a variety of styles; however, it doesn't work when those styles are totally unrelated or incongruous. If your taste leans more toward period decorating, the details you choose should be appropriate for the specific historical style. Fortunately, most traditional architectural details have been around for so long that they've been adapted for many dif-

ferent styles. Columns, for example, are typically classical features but can be found in such divergent settings as Georgian, Victorian, and contemporary interiors.

Other important considerations are size and proportion. The best way to get the most out of an architectural detail is to give it the right amount of space. Within the proper setting, a detail becomes a room highlight that looks like an integral part of the house; in the wrong space, even a good piece can be overwhelming and obtrusive or, on the other hand, disproportionately small and insignificant.

TRIM TIP | Neoclassical Style

Neoclassical is a common decorating term used to describe any style or decoration that follows classical Greek or Roman styling. Georgian, Federal, Greek Revival, and to some extent, Colonial Revival styles all may be loosely described as neoclassical.

An Overview of Architectural Styles

The principal movements in American architecture that are now considered "traditional" span from the early colonial period up to the middle of the 20th century. All of the styles informed both interior and exterior home design.

As artistic movements, the styles inspired the creation or popular adaptation of many of the same architectural details available to homeowners today. A mark of good architectural design is that a home's interior detailing reflects the character of the exterior, and vice versa. Keeping this in mind, a lot can be learned about the spirit of each style and its characteristic architectural details.

GEORGIAN (1700–1780)

In many ways the Georgian period of architecture and interior design represents the introduction of formal architecture in America. While previously colonists built and decorated their homes based on designs from their native countries, the Georgian style was the first to cross regional and ethnic boundaries, appearing in homes along the New England seacoast, on southern plantations, and in backcountry farming areas throughout the colonies. Like many of the important movements that followed, Georgian style was popular in England before making its way across the Atlantic.

Georgian Style. The exterior of a typical Georgian home was stately and symmetrical with a flat facade that conveyed a sense of strength and weight. Georgian interiors reflected the strength and balance of the exterior designs but with greater elegance and a lighter touch. Vertical columns and pilasters and ornate plaster wall and ceiling moldings established strong linear patterns. Ceiling treatments ranged from flat plaster, often painted in yellow, gray, or pink to

Libraries and well-appointed drawing rooms, left, were common in large Georgian homes. This modern room employs many period details, such as the heavy cornice, bookshelves with "Georgian" arches, and a classical bracketed mantelshelf.

A detailed look at classical Georgian features, above, reveals a mantelshelf supported by dentil and egg-and-dart moldings, a nicely proportioned overmantel with broken pediment, and a classic dentil cornice.

evoke a feeling of open sky, to elaborately coffered ceilings or embellishments of ornate plasterwork or trompe l'oeil painting. Throughout the decor, classical ornamentation was the standard: doorways trimmed with pilasters and pediments or entablatures; bold cornices with dentil or Greek key patterns; columns dividing rooms; and motifs of flowered festoons, scrolls, urns, and vases.

Fireplace Designs. Fireplaces were adorned with classical details. Typical elements included egg-and-dart molding, a narrow mantelshelf supported by brackets or molding, and an overmantel. It was common to hang a picture or lean a gilt-frame mirror above the mantle. Many fireplaces were flanked by built-in bookcases trimmed with molding to match other room decor.

Well-integrated trim details were an important design requirement in Georgian interiors.

FEDERAL (1790–1830)

To the casual observer, the exterior of a Federal-style home seems quite similar to a Georgian home, but there are differences. Federal-style homes often include a fan-light window over the entry, full-height pilasters at the corners, and a portico supported by columns around the front door. With its red brick or clapboard walls and charming window shutters, a Federal home embodies a more American aspect when compared with a Georgian's English style, and is commonly described as appearing more "colonial." The Federal style relies on classical Greek and Roman principles of design. The style coincided with the birth of a nation, and evidence of the revered classical principles can be found on the White House, the U.S. Capitol, and state capitols throughout the country.

Room Styles. Despite the perfect symmetry of their exteriors, Federal interiors were made up of rooms of various sizes and shapes. Following the dictates of the occupants' needs rather than a rigid layout, oval and even round rooms were common. The classical details of a Georgian interior—stout columns and bold cornices—become more refined in Federal decorating, with slender columns or pilasters supporting graceful elliptical arches

Architects of the Federal style, above, experimented with room shapes and floor plans to create dynamic yet well-balanced interiors.

A leaded fanlight, opposite, and beautifully molded arch create an elegant Federal entryway.

and wall friezes that were patterned on botanical themes.

Interiors. Federal interiors were light and airy, with high ceilings and larger windows than found in earlier homes. The elegant designs of Scottish architect Robert Adam dominated interior ornamentation. His themes included garlands and delicate swags, rosettes, urns, sunbursts, and ornate plasterwork designs that fanned out in perfect symmetry over a wall or ceiling. Fireplaces were adorned with low-relief carvings, miniature columns, and delicate Adamesque motifs. Ceilings held medallions, often as the center of a painted or applied-plaster design. Wallpaper depicting classical or pastoral scenes became increasingly popular and available. Because interior shutters were common, windows had purely decorative treatments—fringed fabric draped over poles—or none at all. This added to the overall lightness of the interiors, as did the white painted door and window molding.

GREEK REVIVAL (1820–1860)

An extremely popular style in America, Greek Revival sang the praises of democracy through the architecture of ancient Greece. Buildings designed in the purest sense of the style had the single aesthetic goal of mimicking a Greek temple. Homes were fronted by two-story porticos with massive columns; windows were set back from facades and chimneys were kept unobtrusive (Greek temples didn't have windows or fireplaces); wooden pilasters were embedded into exterior walls, and everything paintable was made white to resemble the marble or stone of a temple.

Other exterior elements included a pediment, either on an end gable or over an entry; low-pitched roof; dentil molding; and whitewashed clapboard or stucco siding. Even today, many suburban homes carry modest gable cornice returns made to simulate a pediment, a faint echo of Greek Revival styling.

Simple Interiors. Inside these American "temples" the decor typically was simpler and less ornate than in Federal and Georgian interiors. Walls were usually adorned only with a baseboard, though often large, and with crown or cornice molding, the wall field between painted or papered in organic hues such as stone, soft pastel, deep pink, gray, or terra cotta. Ceilings often carried little more than a medallion and flat paint treatment. Tall windows, sometimes reaching to the floor, and doors were trimmed with fairly plain reeded or fluted molding, while window treatments were often elaborate and ornamental. Richly colored window hangings swagged between gilt rosettes were purely for ornament, while sheer lace or muslin undercurtains allowed soft, diffuse light into the rooms. In grand homes, pier glasses—floor-to-ceiling mirrors installed between two windows—were a common feature.

Materials of Choice. Not surprisingly, marble and stone were considered the height of Grecian style. Fine interiors featured stone or marble for the flooring in grand entrance halls, as well as in baseboards and door surrounds with carved lintels. White and black marble fireplace surrounds typified the pared-down opulence of post-and-lintel temple design. In more modest homes, mantels and other architectural details were made of wood and painted to look like marble.

This contemporary bathroom, left, makes obvious references to ancient construction, from the pediment over the mirror to the keyed archway above the shower door.

Simple wall and ceiling decoration, clean styling, and sober colors characterize a Greek Revival interior, opposite top.

A combination of grandiose forms and basic stone materials captures the spirit of classical architecture, opposite bottom.

VICTORIAN (1840–1900)

The Victorian era was named for England's Queen Victoria, who ruled Britain from 1837 to 1901. In both Britain and America, the period was a time of great economic growth, population expansion, increased industrialization, and the growth of the middle class. Stylistically, it was an age of romance and eclecticism. After a century and a half of logical and orderly neoclassical design, Victorian style burst forth with its ideals of abundance, imagination, and diverse cultural richness.

In American popular architecture, the broad heading of "Victorian" includes four main house styles—gothic revival, Italianate, Second Empire, and Queen Anne among others. Each style has distinctive exterior characteristics.

Victorian Interiors. The history of Victorian interior decoration does not fall easily into distinct categories, but it does reveal an evolution over its long life. What was common among all Victorian decorators was their love of ornament. In varying degrees, rooms were adorned with architectural details made of plaster, stone, wrought iron, hand-crafted glass, and most commonly, dark-stained

Many Victorian details, above, were factory-produced, making elaborate decorations affordable to a broader public, although quality was often secondary to appearance.

Victorians drew liberally from other decorative styles, as shown at right by the classical columns and corbels (supporting the ceiling arches).

A view through several areas, opposite, reveals the "anything goes" nature of some Victorian decorating. Picture rails, cornices, and boldly profiled door molding were typical details.

woods such as oak and mahogany. Ceilings were almost always bordered by a bold cornice, their interior spaces covered with decorative plasterwork, coffers, tin tiles, or colorful paint or paper treatments. A popular wall treatment was a tripartite arrangement in which a baseboard, chair rail, and picture rail created three distinct areas, named *dado* (below chair rail), *field* (above chair rail), and *frieze* (between picture rail and cornice). These areas were commonly decorated with a variety of colors or papers in contrasting patterns. Beautiful wallpaper of all descriptions was the primary decorating tool for Victorians.

Decorative Motifs. Throughout Victorian interiors, decorative motifs ranged widely—from classical designs to floral patterns to geometric forms and fleurs-de-lis. Elements of escapism took form in the exotic symbols and styling of Turkish, Moorish, Oriental, Arabian, and Indian cultures. These were also found in exterior elements, such as onion shaped domes, horseshoe arches, and oval openings. Given the inventiveness and exuberance of the Victorian decorator, it's not surprising to find homes with a combination of styles—a Gothic library next to a Moorish parlor, across from an eclectic drawing room.

CRAFTSMAN (1890–1920)

Craftsman style is closely linked to the English Arts and Crafts movement of the mid- to late 1800s, so close that often the terms appear to be used interchangeably. What distinguishes the two is that *Arts and Crafts* primarily describes a style of interior design while *Craftsman*, a term popularized by American designer Gustav Stickley, encompasses interior decoration and the building plan behind the immensely popular American bungalow house. Both movements were highly developed and comprehensive, influencing designs for furniture, glasswork, light fixtures, and even a "Craftsman" lifestyle characterized by simple, healthful living and a respect for nature and indigenous materials. Other associations of Craftsman style are Mission-style furnishings and the work of American architects Greene & Greene and Frank Lloyd Wright, whose shared interest in the organic yet refined forms of traditional Japanese design had a great influence on Arts and Crafts style in America.

Built-ins, below, are a hallmark of Craftsman style. Many were made of quarter-sawn oak, a lumber prized for its stability and beautiful, straight grain.

The open floor plans, opposite, of Craftsman homes require details with a continuity of style.

Craftsman Philosophy. At the core of Craftsman style are the tenets of Arts and Crafts philosophy: traditional craftsmanship over Industrial Age factory production; inherent beauty of natural materials over painted and stylized embellishment; simplicity and harmony of design over eclecticism and excess of ornament. Following a theory of promoting "honesty" in materials and construction, Craftsman homes displayed exposed joints and structural elements, showing traditional techniques such as dovetailing and mortise-and-tenon joinery. Interiors were filled with architectural details of fine wood, the most common types in America being oak, Douglas fir, redwood, and mahogany treated with clear finishes.

Craftsman interiors were open-plan yet extremely cozy: rooms in main living areas were divided by beautiful wood columns; inglenooks and window seats provided warm places for curling up; and richly grained wainscoting and trim helped unify adjoining spaces. Ceilings often carried decorative box-beams, a no-frills decoration representing structural heft. Where walls weren't covered with tall wainscoting, they received paint in earth tones, textile or grasscloth wallcoverings, or wallpaper with nature motifs or medieval pictorials. Probably the most coveted feature of a Craftsman home was the built-in. These fine examples of practical design and the carpenter's craft were found throughout the house, as dining room sideboards, bedroom dressers, hallway linen closets, and beautiful glazed-door book cabinets.

COLONIAL (1600–1783) &
COLONIAL REVIVAL (1880–1940)

Spanning the years from settlement to the end of the American Revolution, the Colonial period is more a historical era than an architectural movement, but the homes built by the earliest Americans have continued to influence residential design for more than three centuries. The first great wave of influence came during the Colonial Revival of the late 1800s, when American sentiment began harkening back to the simpler, more natural home styles and decorations of pre-Industrial and pre-Victorian times.

Colonial Expansion. By the dawn of the suburban housing boom of the 1920s, Colonial Revival style had expanded to include designs based on a variety of colonial prototypes. Among the most popular were the Dutch Colonial house, with its characteristic gambrel roof and

large dormer; and the Cape Cod, an original colonial dwelling that became one of the most common house styles of the twentieth century. Although in fewer numbers, the Garrison and Saltbox houses of New England were also revived, as well as many examples of Spanish Colonial homes in Florida and the southwestern states.

Colonial Spirit. The typical Colonial home had minimal trimwork that usually included simple baseboards and crown moldings, perhaps a chair rail, and simple door

Mixing Styles. By mixing periods and styles liberally, decorators created rooms with rustic farmhouse implements set within grand, neoclassical schemes reminiscent of Georgian and Federal interiors. In short, anything that arrived before 1830 was considered appropriate decor for a Colonial Revival home. Yet inauthentic as some were, Colonial interiors had undeniable charm and a familiar sense of domesticity; their spiritual connection to America's architectural heritage has made Colonial Revival a popular style to this day.

Colonial Revival interiors, opposite, are modeled after refined late-Colonial and post-Revolution homes and often incorporate neoclassical details.

The thorough period reproduction shown left includes authentic Colonial details: rough ceiling beams with plaster infill, wide-plank wall paneling, a mantel tree, and a utilitarian mantelshelf.

Many early American homes were log structures, which means that Colonial-style decorating can be an especially appropriate style for modern log homes, below.

and window trim. Given the austerity of Colonial interiors, Colonial Revivalists chose to decorate their homes in styles that evoked the spirit of early American life rather than create accurate reproductions. The virtues of their ancestors—simplicity, honesty, utility—were represented in whitewashed trim and paneling, and fireplaces accessorized with cooking utensils, guns, powder horns, and handmade silver plates. Spinning wheels and grandfather clocks served as powerful relics of a simpler, slower time.

COUNTRY STYLE

While not a true architectural movement or period, the Country style of decorating harkens back to the architecture and interior settings of early rural homes. Many regions of the world have their own version of a Country style, from Tuscany to Sweden to the Mediterranean. In America, three country styles predominate: English Country, French Country, and most commonly, American Country, although the distinctions between the three are often minimal and there are no standard building types characterizing the styles.

American Country style has many influences, most notably early Colonial homes and the classic American farmhouse. Interior details might include rough timber ceiling beams that mimic the post-and-beam construction of settlers' homes; simple wood trimwork, usually painted; solid-panel wood shutters; practical built-ins, like corner cupboards and recessed storage cabinets; and humble wood mantels or a lone mantelshelf or rough-timber mantel tree. Classical motifs, such as dentils and reeded molding, are not uncommon (because they were considered symbols of refinement in country settings), but they are often modest and unrefined in character.

European Styles. French and English Country styles are somewhat more diverse than the American style, which tends to be more consistently rustic. These styles have many of the same details and decorative effects but can also include finer styling and more lavish and refined ornament. French Country, also known as French Provincial, is based on the interiors of country homes in southern France. Along with rough plaster walls, exposed timbers, and stone or clay tile floors, a French Country decor might feature fine fabrics, elegant moldings, and the highly characteristic toile de Jouy patterns.

English Style. English Country style follows two decorating traditions—that of the humble cottage and that of the landowner's country home. Cottage interiors are humble and cozy to the core. Rough plaster walls and ceilings and painted wood floors are the backdrops for rustic details with honest, well-worn character. The classic English Country home is exceptionally comfortable, even luxurious, but always with a natural, lived-in appearance that seems to have developed over many years. Trimwork and other details are made of heavy, dark wood to complement the robust furnishings and rich fabrics. An abundance of family heirlooms and personal collectibles are displayed on tables and stout wooden bookcases.

A warm Country scheme, opposite, can humble large room proportions, making the space more intimate.

Architectural details, such as the exposed ceiling beams, decorative shelf, and corner cupboard, add an appealing, home-spun feel to the Country interior above.

One of the best things about Country style, right, is that it allows for an eclectic mix of furniture and ornaments.

CHAPTER 2

BASIC TRIMWORK

*T*rim or molding not only hides gaps and dresses up corners, it is often the backbone of a room's design. The types of baseboard, cornice and crown, chair rail molding, and window and door casings you select help define the character of a room and set the stage for the entire decor. Fortunately, there are a variety of styles and designs from which to choose, so you should have no trouble finding the right trimwork to suit your needs. Most of this book deals with more-elaborate architectural details, such as mantels, window seats, and the like, but any architectural detail that you add must complement the basic molding in the room. This chapter covers the types and uses of basic trimwork and will help you select the molding that best suits your interior design.

Use of Trim in Design

The architectural style of your home and your personal taste will play large parts in selecting trim, but there are other considerations that should guide your decision. Above all, the size and scale of the trim should be appropriate for the room. Low ceilings (8 feet or less) have a harder time supporting large cornices than 10- or 12-foot ceilings. Similarly, a small room can be overwhelmed by large, elaborate trimwork, just as a plain, slender molding disappears in a large room. The scale of a molding relates to its profile as well as its size. Deep and heavy detailing creates bold shadow lines and has greater visual presence than a subtle profile.

Coordinating the various moldings with one another and with other room elements lends a sense of balance and unity to a design scheme. Walls with multiple moldings, such as baseboard, chair rail, and crown, will look best if their sizes and scales are proportionate and decorative aspects complementary. Traditional interiors are full of clever relationships between trim details—for example, a fluted door casing that echoes the fluted columns of a room divider.

The style of your home will play a role in trim selection, but trim details should be in proportion to the rest of the room as shown in the setting above.

Stark color contrasts, opposite, highlight the power and beauty of trimwork.

Popular Profiles

Greek and Roman details are a part of so many decorating styles that it's hard to find ornamental trim without some kind of classical design. The ogee shape, for instance, appears on everything from interior trimwork to exterior cornices to milled table edges. Here are some of the basic molding shapes and motifs that have withstood the test of time.

Torus/Astragal

Ovolo

Ogee

Scotia

Reverse Ogee

Bead-and-Reel

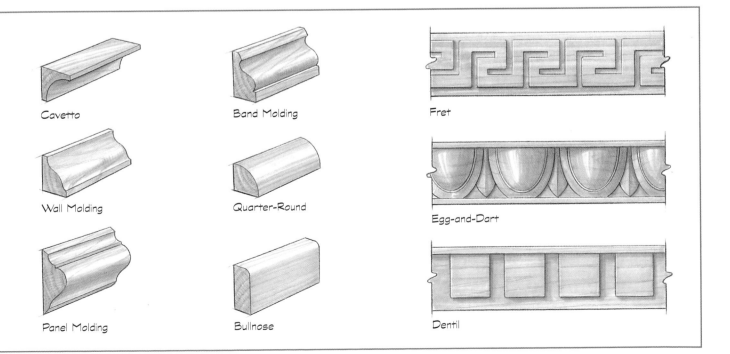

Cavetto

Band Molding

Fret

Wall Molding

Quarter-Round

Egg-and-Dart

Panel Molding

Bullnose

Dentil

SELECTING TRIM MATERIALS

When choosing wood trim, the way you plan to finish the material can help you decide the best material to use. If you plan to paint, you can save money by using a paint-grade softwood, such as pine, poplar, or aspen. Pine is generally the most common and least expensive paint-grade material. When it's available, you can save even more money by choosing finger-jointed stock, which is trim made up of small pieces of wood fused together with finger-like joinery; you can't tell the difference once it's painted. Some styles of paint-grade trim are also available in MDF (medium-density fiberboard) material. MDF trim cuts easily and has a smooth surface, but it's a better material for sheet goods than it is for trim: all cut edges must be moisture-sealed prior to painting, and the material can be damaged by pneumatic nailers.

Natural Finishes. If you prefer to retain the natural beauty of the wood grain with a stain or clear finish, choose trim made from a "clear" (knot-free) softwood or a hardwood such as oak, maple, or cherry. Specialty dealers offer trim in less commonly used species—softwoods like redwood and fir, which were popular for Craftsman interiors, or hardwoods like ash and walnut. For a rustic treatment, you might consider trim made from knotty pine and finished clear or with a diluted whitewash. Regardless of the wood you choose, keep in mind that stain and even clear finishes change the wood's color, so select and test your finish before installing any of the trim.

An additional option for painted or stained trim is synthetic polymer molding. Made of various urethane mate-

Because the owners opted for a classic white finish, above, the designer specified paint-grade softwood moldings, such as pine or poplar.

Natural finishes, opposite, showcase the grain of the wood, so be sure to choose knot-free softwoods or hardwoods for this type of application.

rials, this lightweight trimwork is easy to cut and install and can be painted or stained with a nonpenetrating stain or gel. Though not inexpensive, polymer molding can be an economical option for highly elaborate cornices and other details. Some manufacturers offer flexible polymer molding for trimming around curves.

TRIM TIP | Home Center Trim Departments

Your local home center is a good place to find many standard types of trim. They typically carry pine and poplar for paint-grade work and oak for stain finishes. The material usually comes in 8- or 16-ft. lengths. It is sold by the linear foot, so you can cut down larger pieces to the size you need. Most stores have a hand miter box located in the aisle for anyone to use, or a sales assistant will cut the trim for you.

BASEBOARD

Baseboard hides the gap between the wall and floor and for that reason is present in almost every room of the house. It was developed in the eighteenth century, as owners of grand houses began to prefer plaster walls over wood paneling, and today it remains true to its purpose of protecting wall surfaces from shoes, furniture, and other domestic hazards. As an architectural detail, baseboard provides a foundation to a wall, as a base does to a column, giving the eye a starting point as it absorbs a room's decoration.

Over the years baseboard has diminished in stature if not ubiquity. Georgian and Federal homes had substantial base molding, sometimes made of marble, but always with its detailing in keeping with door and window casing. Victorian and Craftsman decorators also preferred deep baseboards, although with simpler profiles, the latter often favoring a wide, flat board with a slightly rounded top edge. Modern homes typically have narrow ranch- or Colonial-style moldings, sometimes with the same type of trim also used for the window and door casing.

Baseboard provides a foundation for a wall, above, and it should complement the window and door casings.

Baseboard is available in standard one-piece styles. But you can create more ornate built-up looks, such as the design shown at left, by combining standard pieces.

Choosing Baseboard. When choosing baseboard, it's important to make sure it pairs well with the door and window casing. Hold a piece of baseboard against the casing's edge, in the manner they will be installed, to make sure they meet nicely. Sometimes a poor match can be remedied with plinth blocks installed beneath the casing or with a backband added to the casing's outer edge. You'll also need to decide whether to install a base shoe—a slender, usually rounded strip of molding installed along the baseboard's bottom edge. Base shoe is flexible and can follow floor contours to hide gaps left by the baseboard.

Installing Baseboard

Most baseboards require two nails at each stud location. You can also drive nails into the bottom plate. For built-up baseboards, install the main board first, then add the cap and other accent moldings, nailing them into the main board or wall studs. Nail the base shoe to the floor only so that it can move independently of the baseboard and prevent gapping. For outside corners, make miter cuts to connect the molding; for inside corners, make coped cuts. (See chapter 13.) These types of cuts help keep the molding from showing gaps.

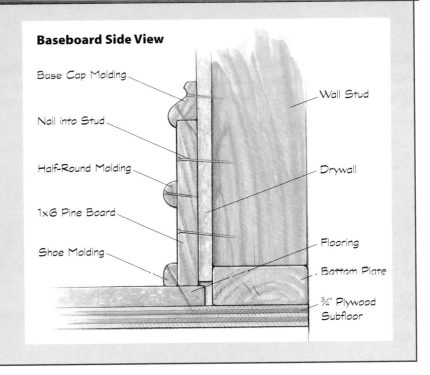

Baseboard Side View

Base Cap Molding

Nail into Stud

Half-Round Molding

1x6 Pine Board

Shoe Molding

Wall Stud

Drywall

Flooring

Bottom Plate

¾" Plywood Subfloor

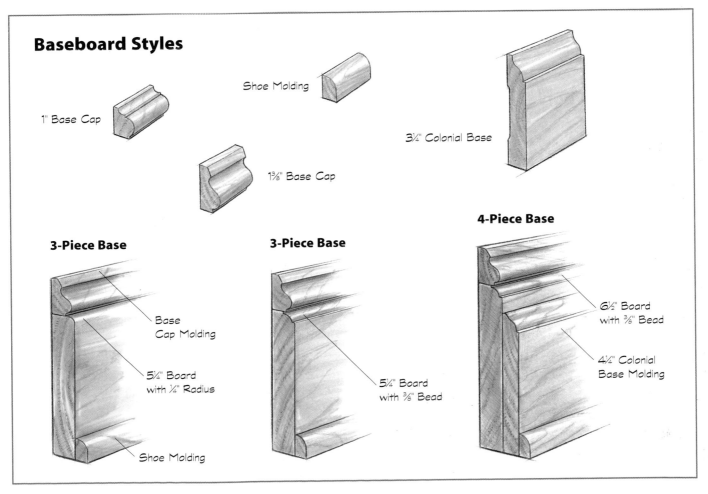

Baseboard Styles

1" Base Cap

Shoe Molding

1⅜" Base Cap

3¼" Colonial Base

3-Piece Base

Base Cap Molding

5¼" Board with ¼" Radius

Shoe Molding

3-Piece Base

5¼" Board with ⅜" Bead

4-Piece Base

6½" Board with ⅜" Bead

4¼" Colonial Base Molding

CROWN MOLDING & CORNICES

Crown moldings and cornices have adorned interiors since the advent of the plastered ceiling. By concealing and dressing up the joint where walls meet ceilings, these moldings do more than any other to eliminate boxiness in an untrimmed room.

Crown. In architectural nomenclature, crown generally refers to the types of single-piece molding that are installed at an angle to their adjoining surfaces. As its name indicates, crown molding serves as an ornamental capping to walls, cabinets, and built-ins, but is also useful as a decorative support for horizontal elements, such as a fireplace mantelshelf. A simpler trim, similar to crown molding and usually with a concave profile, is called cove molding.

Cornices. The term "cornice" describes large, one-piece molding installed along the top of a wall or above a window, or the same treatment made from multiple pieces of trim, also called a built-up cornice.

Traditionally, cornices and crowns reflected the type and intended use of the rooms they decorated. Reception rooms and primary bedrooms typically had ornate cornice treatments, while kitchens and other functional areas carried much plainer detailing. Over the years cornices and crowns have become much smaller, but most still bear the shapes of their Greco-Roman origins. Combining these traditional shapes to create a unique trim detail is not only an economical option for modern decorators; it's a challenge relished by interior designers.

Installing Crowns and Cornices. Installation can be tricky, and for do-it-yourselfers installation is an important consideration when choosing a molding. Chapter 13 illustrates the basic cuts involved, which are difficult due to the molding's angle. Generally, the larger the molding and the more elaborate the detailing, the harder it is to install, especially if the material is wood. Built-up cornices, because they consist of simpler, smaller pieces, are easier to install than one-piece versions of similar complexity. Some polymer crown and cornice moldings are available with decorative corner blocks that eliminate difficult corner cuts. In any case, painting the molding instead of staining allows you to hide small gaps and other imperfections with caulk before covering it with paint.

This Victorian detail, top, shows how relatively simple crown molding acts as a transition piece between the wall and ceiling designs.

A dentiled cornice, above, with strong visual character nicely carries a vibrant ceiling treatment.

Adding crown molding to the corner cabinet below provides a built-in appearance.

Installing Crown Molding

Installing crown molding often requires more than one method. Along walls that are perpendicular to the ceiling joists, nail the crown to the wall studs and ceiling joists. On walls parallel with the joists, there's usually no joist where you need it. One solution is to install triangular nailing blocks before running the molding—fasten the blocks to the studs or top plates; then fasten the molding to the blocks.

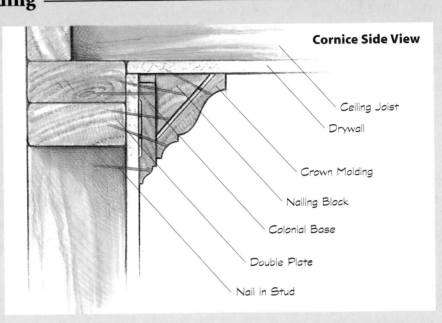

Cornice Side View

Ceiling Joist

Drywall

Crown Molding

Nailing Block

Colonial Base

Double Plate

Nail in Stud

Crown & Cornice Styles

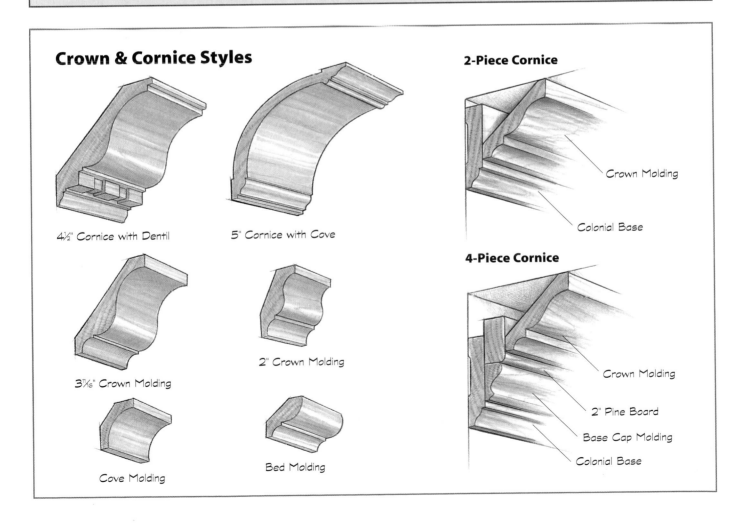

4½" Cornice with Dentil

5" Cornice with Cove

3⅞" Crown Molding

2" Crown Molding

Cove Molding

Bed Molding

2-Piece Cornice

Crown Molding

Colonial Base

4-Piece Cornice

Crown Molding

2" Pine Board

Base Cap Molding

Colonial Base

CHAIR RAIL, PICTURE RAIL & FRIEZES

Chair rail, picture rail, and friezes are horizontal wall moldings that, while less common than baseboard and crown molding, have been popular features of many house styles and have rather interesting origins and functions.

Chair Rail. Also called dado rail, chair rail is installed about waist-high and originally was used to protect walls from chair backs and other furniture. Today, it remains a common detail in more-traditional interiors, offering the decorating effects of providing a focal point and helping to unify the various room details, such as door and window trim and fireplace surrounds. Chair rail often serves as a cap for a wainscot of wood paneling or wallpaper.

Picture Rail and Frieze Molding. These types of moldings have a similar visual effect, both being installed about one-quarter to one-half of the way down a wall from the ceiling. When run around the perimeter of a room, these moldings create a space above known as a frieze, which is often decorated in a manner distinct from the wall space below. The difference between the two moldings is that picture rail has a rounded top edge that projects from the wall and is designed to receive special hooks for hanging pictures. Friezes typically are flat moldings with decorative relief carving or a classical profile. They are most common in homes that follow neoclassical styling. An interesting hybrid of picture rail and frieze was developed by the Shakers, who adorned their exceptionally plain and practical interiors with a pegged frieze, something like a continuous coat rack, and hung from it tools, mirrors, coats, and even furniture.

TRIM TIP   Custom Profiles

When your trim needs go beyond the standard selections available through home centers and lumberyards, a custom millwork shop, mail-order outlet, or Internet site that caters to woodworkers should do the trick. These sources can often help you design a custom profile or can match a sample of old trim that you provide.

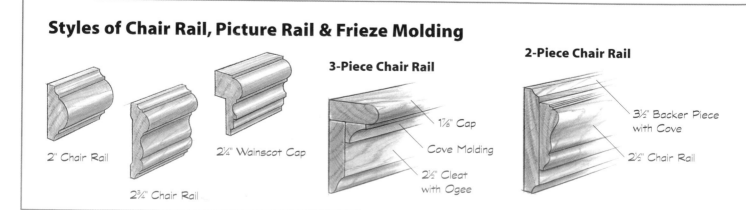

Styles of Chair Rail, Picture Rail & Frieze Molding

2" Chair Rail

2¾" Chair Rail

2¼" Wainscot Cap

3-Piece Chair Rail

1⅛" Cap

Cove Molding

2½" Cleat with Ogee

2-Piece Chair Rail

3½" Backer Piece with Cove

2½" Chair Rail

2

BASIC TRIMWORK

should be coped at inside corners and mitered at outside corners.

A third type of rail, the plate rail, was a popular detail in Colonial and Craftsman homes. Intended for displaying plates at eye level or higher, plate rails have a narrow shelf with a continuous groove for holding a plate's edge, and may be supported below by crown molding or wood brackets.

Picture rail, opposite, can hang at any height that works for your room. The rail shown serves as an edging for a wallpaper border above.

Coved cornice molding and a high frieze band, left, create a unique cove detail.

Wood-paneled wainscoting with a chair rail cap, below, adds traditional detailing that's appropriate for almost any style.

Tripartite. Combining chair rail and picture rail or frieze on the same wall creates three distinct wall fields—an arrangement known by decorators as tripartite. A Victorian-style wall treatment, the tripartite detailing expands the decorating opportunities, allowing you to panel, paint, or paper each field separately for a unique combination. These moldings are simple to install, requiring one or two finish nails at each wall-stud location. Shaped molding

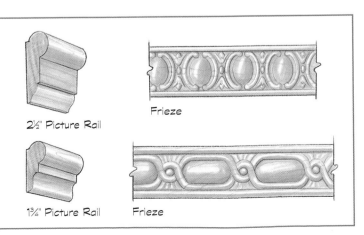

2½" Picture Rail

Frieze

1¾" Picture Rail

Frieze

Door & Window Casing

Casing is the trim that surrounds door and window openings and hides the gap between the wall finish and the jambs of the door or window frame. In most homes, both today and historically, the same casing is used for the doors and windows, although main entry doors often carry different embellishment from internal doors. Casing plays an important and unique decorative role because it frames passages, thereby affecting the view of what lies beyond the passage, just as a picture frame contributes to the visual impact of the painting it contains.

Most casing styles can be grouped into one of two broad categories: tapered and square. Tapered casing is heaviest along its outside edge and tapers toward the edge that contacts the door or window jamb. Because of its taper, this type of casing is almost always installed with mitered corners (like a picture frame). Square casing has the same thickness on both sides and, if not smooth, has symmetrical detailing across its face. Square casing can be mitered at the corners or can be combined with decorative corner blocks and plinth blocks, adding visual weight and substance to the treatment.

Door casing, above, helps define the style of the entry. Here, a traditional profile is paired with a panel door and brass lockset.

Although simple in design, the hefty window casings shown below help tie together all of the trim elements in this room.

Installing Door & Window Casing

The first step to installing casing is establishing the reveal: the narrow strip of jamb that is left exposed when the casing is installed. Without a reveal, it will look as if you're trying to make the jamb and casing appear as one piece, but unsuccessfully. Most reveals are about $\frac{1}{8}$ inch. When you decide what looks best, make light pencil marks representing the reveal on each jamb at the corners of the opening; use these marks for your measurements.

To install mitered casing, cut the casing pieces and temporarily tack them in place, then make sure the joints fit tightly before permanently attaching the casing. Nail the casing to the jamb edges with small (4d or so) finish nails; then nail through the outer edges of the casing into the wall framing, using 6d finish nails.

If you're using corner and plinth blocks, install them first, then cut the casing to fit in between. It usually looks best if the casing is slightly narrower than the blocks, creating reveals on those pieces as well as along the jambs.

Butted Casing with Mitered Backband

Butted Casing with Reveal

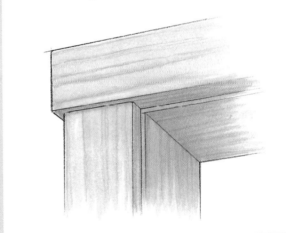

Mitered Casing
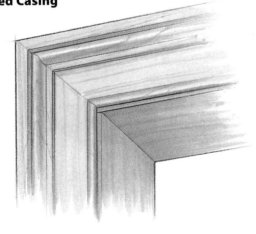

Casing with Corner Blocks

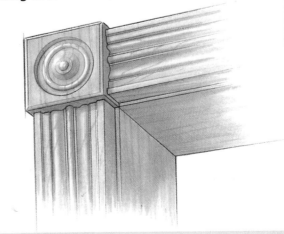

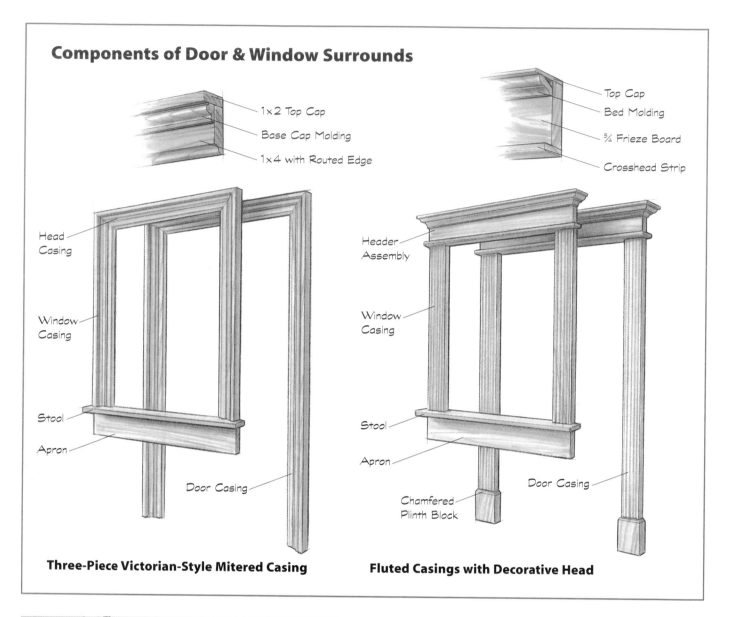

Components of Door & Window Surrounds

1×2 Top Cap
Base Cap Molding
1×4 with Routed Edge

Top Cap
Bed Molding
¾ Frieze Board
Crosshead Strip

Head Casing

Header Assembly

Window Casing

Window Casing

Stool

Stool

Apron

Apron

Door Casing

Chamfered Plinth Block

Door Casing

Three-Piece Victorian-Style Mitered Casing

Fluted Casings with Decorative Head

Header Treatments. In addition to casing, doors and windows in older homes often carried attractive header treatments. Classical pediments were a common detail in homes from the Georgian through the Colonial Revival periods; now they're available through millwork and architectural product dealers. Even more popular is the frieze header based on classical entablatures, consisting of a broad, horizontal frieze board topped with crown and

The corner brackets shown on the window at left embellish an otherwise simple window casing.

Ornate header treatments, such as the pediment opposite, are available through millwork shops.

other moldings. Variations of the frieze header are still common today, and they're surprisingly easy to make using stock lumber and standard molding.

Window trimwork typically matches that of doors, but windows have four sides rather than three and thus present more options for embellishment. The simple window surround most common in modern homes consists of tapered casing along all four sides of the window. A more

traditional style is the stool-and-apron treatment, whereby a flat, horizontal stool, or sill, projects out from the window an inch or more beyond the wall surface, creating a small shelf. The stool ends are notched to fit around the wall and have extensions called horns that meet the bottom ends of the vertical casing. An apron—a flat board, usually of the same material as the stool but often thinner—finishes the underside of the stool.

C H A P T E R   3

WINDOW SEATS

A cozy seat at a window is a cherished place. Bright and embracing, window seats invite you to sit and read a book, take an afternoon nap, or do nothing more than gaze out at the view. And when you consider how much they can improve a space, it's not surprising that window seats are popular. In cramped rooms, window seats provide not only economical seating but much-needed storage space, while in larger, less personal areas, a window seat can be a semiprivate nook from which a sitter can turn attention to either the window or the activity in the room. Typically, window seats are built into wall alcoves or recesses made by bay windows, but other applications can be just as effective. For example, you can create an alcove by using bookshelves or cabinets.

Window Seats & Design

The look of the window seat has changed somewhat over the years—to decorators of the Georgian period a window seat was a miniature backless sofa set into a window recess—but its concept and design benefits have remained true. In addition to its function as a private getaway for one person, a window seat helps a common room work more effectively for groups by offering a convenient place for a few people to sit and talk while remaining connected to the gathering. Window seats are also "human" in scale, meaning that their dimensions fit the body well and provide a sense of comfort, as contrasted with the impersonal and imposing scale of a great room with a 20-foot ceiling.

Window seats are versatile by design. And because they accommodate the basic human need to sit and the considerable modern need for storage, they have been adapted for use in all types of rooms. But not all window seats have to include storage space or even be good for sitting. Some of the most attractive window seats are topped with bare wood shelves that hold decorative items or are left empty to emphasize the window's glow.

The attic window seat below makes the most of an unusual space. While the actual windows are low and short, the seat, trompe l'oeil fanlight, and drapery swags give the entire alcove an aspect of a window.

As period features, window seats are appropriate for almost any interior style but were favored most by the Craftsman movement and the builders of the bungalow house. The window seat is a perfect example of Craftsman design: it is practical, it integrates a house with its furnishings, and it connects the homeowner with the outdoors. Unlike standard furniture pieces, which are merely contents of a room, window seats are built-in details that soften the feel of a home's structure and make a space inherently more inviting.

Planning a Window Seat

As evidenced by their many styles and configurations, there's no standard method for building window seats. The essential design consists of a box-like frame topped with a sturdy seat board and usually a cushion for comfort. Simple versions might have only a front panel and a lid supported by cleats nailed to a wall on either side. A great do-it-yourself design uses ordinary kitchen cabinets for the box and offers the advantage of automatic storage space with convenient front access. (See "Building Window Seats," on pages 54–55.) Following are several important considerations to address when planning your own window seat.

OVERALL DIMENSIONS

The dimensions of the seat alcove have a lot to do with how a seat gets used. For example, a reading alcove made for one person should be a cozy space where the reader feels embraced by the surroundings, much as one feels on a good couch. When a seat is intended for more than one person, make sure there is enough room for everyone to lean back comfortably. Sitting so that everyone faces the room, with their backs against the wall underneath the window, helps accommodate more people.

Another factor contributing to the feel of a window seat is the ceiling height. A simple soffit frame can lower the ceiling height a few inches to enhance the embracing quality of the alcove. This also adds visual definition to the space, giving it more architectural importance in the room. A soffit can hold recessed light fixtures that provide downlighting for reading.

Part window seat, part restaurant booth, the eating area shown above demonstrates the efficiency of built-in seating.

Long and formal the seat at right provides an elegant foundation that emphasizes the high windows. Short columns below and a round head pillow add touches of classical styling.

SEAT DIMENSIONS

The size and height of the sitting surface are critical to the comfort of a window seat. The depth of the seat (from the front edge to the window) should be at least 22 inches, with the same width for the back support. Angled sides add comfort for sitting, but if there's only enough room for vertical sides, you can compensate with plump pillows. Any additional depth you can afford will make the seat feel more roomy and provide space for setting down books or a cup of tea. But a seat that is too deep will make it difficult to lean back in comfort. For napping on the seat, plan on a seat that is 30 to 36 inches deep.

DECOR TIP | Comfort Levels

You may need to take steps to improve the comfort level around the window. Shades, blinds, or some other type of window treatment will come in handy if the window receives direct sun. For drafty windows, consider installing weather stripping or a sash replacement kit before adding the window seat.

Seat Width. To plan the width of the seat (from side to side), take into account everyone who will use it and for what purposes. A minimum width for an average-size person seated parallel with the window is about 36 inches. Seats intended for napping or overnight sleeping must be at least as wide as the tallest sleeper's height, plus several inches to accommodate blankets and pillows. For architectural balance, a window seat should be at least 8 to 12 inches wider than the window. This allows room for trimwork or other decoration without crowding the window.

Seat Height. As for the height of the seat, a good starting point is 15 inches above the floor. With a good, thick cushion, this puts the seat height even with a standard chair or bench. A few inches of variation either way shouldn't cause a problem. However, keep in mind that taller seats can be less inviting because they appear to require more effort to use as a seat, while low seats can make one feel uncomfortably close to the floor.

COMFORT

A good cushion makes all the difference for a window seat. For comfort and durability, choose a cushion with a medium to firm foam core covered with cotton batting. Most cushions start at about 3 inches in thickness. The fabric quality is also important. For durability, use upholstery-grade material. In kitchens or other areas where the cushion is likely to get dirty, apply a stain-resistant treatment or choose vinyl or laminated fabric. The cushion fabric should also be fade-resistant if the seat will get a lot of direct sunlight. A zipper at the back will make the cushion cover easy to remove for washing.

Sitting directly in front of a window can be much hotter or colder than sitting elsewhere in the room. And the fact is, your seat won't be used much if it's too hot or cold for comfort. Also, the quality and intensity of sunlight at various times of the day affects how a seat is used, as well as the general ambiance of the space.

Bench-style window seats, opposite, can accommodate more people by facing them into the room. This comfortable seat still allows one person to sit with their feet up and lean against the side wall.

A charming variation on the standard window seat, this bench at right fills a windowed alcove with enough seats for an intimate group.

STORAGE

Storage space is a great secondary benefit of a window seat, but it's important that the space and access suit your needs, or the space will go unused. The classic flip-up seat lid offers bin-style storage and top access with less bending, but you must remove the cushions to get to the lid.

On the other hand, front-access, cabinet-style storage requires more bending, but you never have to take off the cushions. In general, cabinet storage provides better organization of stored items. Doors mounted to the front of the seat can be any style, including hinged, sliding, or removable panel, or you can omit the doors altogether. A third option is using drawers that pull out from the front. Drawer fronts can be made less conspicuous than most cabinet doors, but adding them usually requires a custom design, and they are more expensive to build than doors.

The low, cozy seat at right strikes a nice balance with the imposing scale of this built-in and ceiling-high window. Drawers can be a stylish option for utilizing under-seat storage space.

Window seats, opposite top, often interfere with baseboard heaters, but moving the unit to the front of the seat is an easy project for an electrician or heating contractor.

Cushioned and pillowed, opposite bottom, a radiator cover has the decorative effect of a window seat and even provides a perch for a quick rest.

UTILITIES

Baseboard heaters, radiators, and air registers are often placed under windows, which presents a problem for installing a window seat. If you have electric or hot-water baseboard heaters, discuss the situation with a contractor. In most cases, the heating unit can simply be moved to the front side of the seat. Short radiators are sometimes covered with ventilated, removable window seats, which, if designed properly, can actually improve the radiator's heating efficiency. Dealing with hot-air registers is easier: typically, you can add a duct extension to the existing ductwork and connect it to a new register (grill) mounted to the front of the window seat.

Building Window Seats

The best cabinets to use for a window seat are the short wall units designed for installation over a refrigerator. At 15 inches tall and 24 inches deep, these cabinets are good building blocks for using as is or as a base that will have a few inches added here or there as needed. If your window seat will go into an existing alcove, the cabinets should fit fairly well, but you can always hide gaps at the sides using filler boards. Home centers carry stock cabinets (the cheapest option), or you can order semicustom cabinets (more expensive but with better selection) from a cabinet showroom. In either case, try to match the cabinet door styles and finishes to any other cabinetry in the room.

Building the Frame. Following the basic installation shown here, start with a 2x4 base built to match the width of the alcove, and fasten it to the floor and wall so that the base is perfectly level and its front edge is flush with the cabinet face-frame. For a taller seat, use 2x6 lumber for the base. Center the cabinet over the base, and secure it with screws driven into the wall and base. If there are multiple

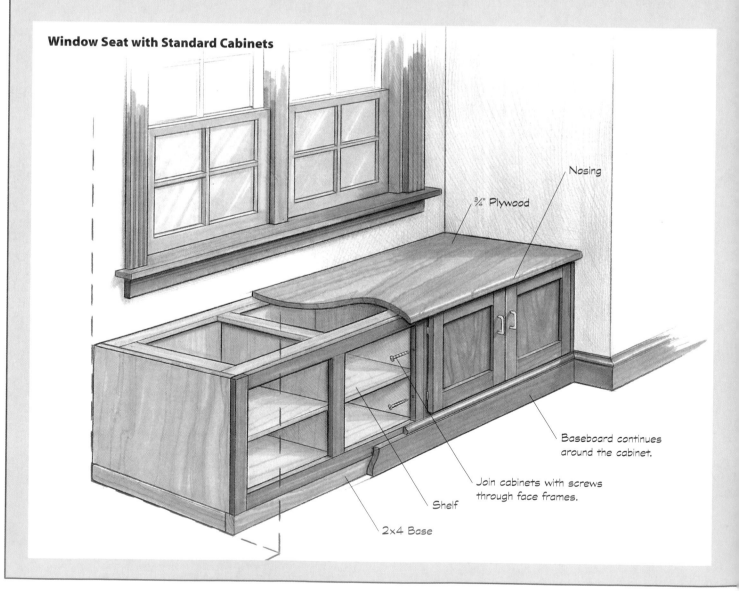

Window Seat with Standard Cabinets

¾" Plywood

Nosing

Baseboard continues around the cabinet.

Join cabinets with screws through face frames.

Shelf

2x4 Base

cabinets, screw them together through the face frames before installing. If necessary, cut filler boards from material that matches the cabinets and install them by screwing through the face frames.

To create an alcove, use pantry kitchen cabinets to flank the window seat as shown below.

Cut the Seat. Make a seat from ¾-inch plywood that has a veneer that matches the cabinet, or use MDF if you plan to paint the seat. The seat should fit tight to all of the walls. Finish the front edge of the seat with nosing trim or iron-on veneer tape. Secure the seat to the top cabinet edges using construction adhesive.

Final Touches. Finish by adding baseboard and other trim to hide the window seat base, and apply caulk or small trim to cover any large gaps along the seat or filler boards.

Window Seat with Kitchen Pantry Cabinets

Crown Molding

¾" Plywood with Nosing

Toe Kick

Locating a Window Seat

Window seats can go anywhere in the house, provided there's an available window, of course. One of the best places is in a corner where windows meet. This is an out-of-the-way space that allows for a large, L-shaped seat and views in two directions. If you can afford the space, hallways and stair landings can benefit from the leisure qualities of a window seat, giving these traffic areas the comfortable look of a living space.

Practical Matters. When it comes to choosing a room in which to install a window seat, consider the seat's practical attributes as well as its decorative benefits. Kitchens

DECOR TIP | Creating Space

Mudrooms are ideal locations for simple, practical window seats with plenty of storage space: a flip-up seat offers a place for putting on boots while storing hats, gloves, and dog leashes underneath. For even more storage space, combine a window seat with built-in cabinets or shelves. If located adjacent to the kitchen, a mudroom with extra storage can also serve as a pantry.

get-togethers and acting as relatively private spaces within generally public areas. The way you size, configure, and decorate the seat can emphasize one or the other of those purposes. A wide seat with cushions along the window wall can be used as a sofa, while a well-defined alcove, perhaps with a lowered ceiling, is better suited for one person. If you want guests to feel comfortable plopping down on the seat, don't make it too formal or display-like.

A small dormer alcove, opposite, would usually be wasted space. Adding a window seat turns it into a functional part of the room.

The expansive landing shown at left has plenty of room for a window seat, which creates a comfortable atmosphere and visually helps to ground the oversize window.

Even the simplest of seats, below, can be highly effective. This spare design dresses up the radiator without restricting airflow and creates a one-of-a-kind relaxation and reading area.

are natural places for window seats, especially when they're used for bench-style seating at a dining table. A long seat can hold lots of kids and eliminate the sliding of chairs in and out. Window seats also require less floor space than chairs. Under-seat spaces can store seldom-used kitchen items, like picnic supplies, tablecloths, and holiday trays.

Bedroom Window Seats. These offer the ultimate in privacy, the perfect place to read or take a nap. Here you can decorate the seat any way you like and never have to worry about tidying up. A seat also comes in handy for putting on shoes or laying out clothes.

Kids love window seats in their bedrooms for all of these reasons. Even more than adults, they're naturally drawn to private, sheltered places good for daydreaming and gazing outdoors—and having a window seat in a child's own room makes it a much more personal space.

In family rooms and living rooms, window seats often serve the dual purposes of providing additional seating for

Bay Window Seats

One way to add a window seat, even in a place where there's no window, is to install a new bay window unit. Bay windows are striking architectural details that add a great deal of light to an interior and a great deal of character both inside and out—not to mention expansive views from the window seat. And all of this comes with no loss of floor space.

Newer bay windows are much improved over their predecessors. Where older bays required support from exterior brackets, extended floor joists, or a foundation bump-out, newer models use an internal cable system that anchors to the wall framing and eliminates the need for external supports. This means you can install a bay in any wall or story of your house without major framing reconstruction. However, adding such a window is still too difficult a job for the average do-it-yourselfer.

The classic bay window style has three faces. The front face is parallel with the wall, and the sides are set at angles—either 30, 45, or 60 degrees—to the front. Common variations on the classic style include the bow window, which has a rounded projection, and the box window, with a square shape and often without windows at the sides. Many styles of bays (as well as bows and boxes) are available with built-in seats in natural wood finishes. A fitted cushion and some pillows are all you need to add for a cozy seat with an incredible view. When planning the installation, make sure to position the window so that the seat will be at a comfortable height.

Window seats, above, are great for informal dining areas, where family members like to gather at all times of the day.

Bay windows, opposite, are ideal for window seats. Today's bay units have internal support systems, and some have built-in seats. Smaller versions can be installed in standard window openings.

CHAPTER 4

WINDOW CORNICES
& SHUTTERS

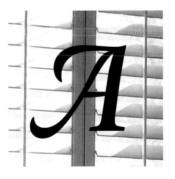

A s the principal architectural details for windows, cornices and shutters provide both functional and aesthetic benefits. Cornices can be an attractive addition to a variety of window treatments and are an especially good choice for covering multilayered hangings that require a lot of hardware. Building your own cornice is a great do-it-yourself project because you can use standard, inexpensive materials for the basic unit and cover it with almost any finish, including paint or stain, wallpaper, fabric, and molding. Playing a very different role from cornices, shutters have remained timeless window features for both practical and decorative reasons: they block cold air in winter and solar heat in summer; they provide privacy while allowing soft lines of light to play over an interior space.

Cornices

Cornices first appeared in the sixteenth century in France, though they were not commonly used in America until the Georgian period of the 1800s, when simple curtains gave way to full-length draperies as standard window coverings. Because they conceal the bunched ends of drapery, as well as all the hanging hardware, cornices add a finished look to window treatments, but they can do much more. Their sturdy frames make a good foundation for hanging additional embellishment, such as lambrequins, or for supporting ornate molding treatments. They also help define the proportions of a window, emphasizing its architectural role within a room. Drawing the eye upward to the top of the window—an area that's usually ignored—cornices effectively adorn the blank wall area between the window and ceiling.

The simple cornice below adds to a pleasing mix of geometric shapes and active swirls. A little paint highlights the box's trim detail and provides a distinct frame for the painted design within.

The carved cornice shown to the right softens the overall feel created by the sharp angles and hard surfaces of this modern kitchen.

DECORATING TIPS

As a top treatment, a cornice has an impact on everything below, whether it's a layered fabric, simple curtains, blinds or shades, or a bare, unadorned window. For vertical drapes and shades, cornices provide a strong horizontal element that balances and softens their visual impact. Mini-blinds, roll-up shades, and other practical treatments can present a special decorating challenge, but by adding a cornice, you can hide the unattractive tops of blinds or shades while visually linking the treatments to the overall room decor. A deep cornice can completely hide retracted blinds.

Different window types can benefit from specific cornice designs. A narrow window can be made to appear wider by extending a cornice well beyond the sides of the window and hanging full-length drapes down the sides. Deep cornices can add perceived height to short windows. And plain, modern windows can borrow character from cornices with decorative front panels. Where separate windows are grouped, a continuous cornice draws the windows together and simplifies the hanging of drapery.

Period Designs. Cornices also offer great opportunities for incorporating period motifs. Any one of the many classical designs, such as swags, garland, or classical mold-

ing details, will add the right touch to a neoclassical interior. Victorian decorating, particularly during the late 1800s, made much of window treatments, often covering cornices with rich, boldly patterned fabrics and fringe. For a Gothic Revival scheme, a dark wood cornice with pointed-arch cutouts evokes the appropriate feel of a medieval church.

If you're covering your cornice with fabric and want to follow a period style, contact a textile manufacturer that specializes in reproductions. The company will help you find the right fabric for your desired style and can recommend patterns for drapery and other window treatments.

4

WINDOW CORNICES & SHUTTERS

CORNICE CONSTRUCTION

A basic cornice has three sides made of wood or other board material and a top that may serve as a shelf for decorative items. This distinguishes a cornice from a valance, which can vary in design from a three-sided frame with no top to a simple fabric treatment covering the top of drapery. You can build a cornice frame using ordinary materials—one-by lumber, plywood, MDF, even cardboard or mat board—and cover it with fabric, paint, or wallpaper, or add some architectural detailing with molding or carved appliqués. A finer cornice might be made with hardwood panels or scroll-carved brackets for sidepieces. Large crown or cornice molding by itself can make a beautiful cornice with dramatic, angling sides. Wooden cornices often have decoratively shaped bottom edges, which you can make using a paper pattern and a saber saw. For those not interested in building one, cornices are available custom built to your specifications through millwork companies and architectural product dealers.

Mounting the Cornice. Cornices can be mounted to the wall above or beside the window trim or attached directly to the window trim (casing) or frame. For wall-mount installations, a 2×2 lumber nailer or metal L-brackets work well—use these for full-size wooden cornices that have some weight. Lightweight cardboard or mat board versions can be tacked to the window casing.

The ornate Victorian cornice above is actually quite simple in construction. A basic box, papered to match the walls, conceals the drapery tops and serves as a foundation for an interesting piece of trimwork with hanging swags.

Often the cornice box, left, is just the beginning. Here, a fabric lambrequin is used to give this cornice a unique sculptural shape that complements the furnishings.

An elegant, curved cornice, opposite, draws attention away from an oddly shaped room and angled ceiling line. The presence of a single decorative item playfully demonstrates that a cornice can also be used as a shelf.

DESIGNING A CORNICE

If your cornice will cover the tops of other window treatments, it's a good idea to take final measurements and design the cornice after all of the other elements are in place. To determine the width (from side to side) of the cornice, measure the drapery hardware and add 6 to 8 inches. To determine the depth, measure from the wall (or window trim if the cornice will be installed directly to the trim) to the outside front edge of the drapes; then add about 3 inches to ensure that the drapes will move freely behind the front panel. The width and depth dimensions are for the inside of the cornice box. If the cornice will be the only window treatment, size the box based on how you want the cornice to look against the window trim.

The cut bottom edge of the cornice shown above is symmetrical yet cleverly reflects the rumpled look of the window treatment. Its top edge is softened with a bead of rope molding.

For a subtle application, you can install cornices against the ceiling, right, and continue the room's crown molding treatment around the cornices. This adds architectural emphasis to windows without crowding the windows themselves.

Cornice Height. The height of the cornice is a matter of personal preference, but decorators generally recommend a height of 4 to 6 inches plus the width of the casing. Because the height largely determines the overall impact of the cornice, you might want to experiment with different dimensions before deciding. (See the Trim Tip, "Cornice Mock-Up," below.) Too small, and the cornice will look undersized for the window and treatments; too large, and its impact will be overwhelming. Any trimwork you add will increase the visual impact as well. Another consideration is how much the cornice will cover the window. If blocking light is a concern, plan to install the cornice so that its bottom edge is even with the window glass.

Cornices that are wrapped in fabric often have a layer of padding for a slightly pillowed appearance. To achieve this effect, wrap the box with 1-inch-thick fiberfill batting adhered with glue; then cover the batting with a complete layer of muslin fabric, which gives the outer layer of fabric a smooth finish. Finally, add the outer, decorative fabric, securing it with staples along the hidden surfaces of the box. You can wrap the fabric around the inside of the box if it will be visible or paint the insides of the box and finish the fabric edge with decorative trim.

TRIM TIP | Cornice Mock-Up

Build a cardboard prototype of your cornice, and tack or tape it in place to test the design. View the mock-up from different parts of the room to make sure it covers everything you want it to.

Building & Installing a Cornice

A traditional painted cornice like the one shown here starts with a simple wooden box. Cover the box with any combination of molding, fabric, or other decoration. The construction steps are the same for most cornice styles.

Cut the side, top, and front pieces for the box from ¾-inch plywood or MDF, or one-by paint-grade lumber. Plan so that the top piece overlaps the edges of the side and front pieces. If the corner joints will not be covered with molding, fit the side and front pieces together with mitered joints so that no end grain is exposed. Assemble the box with wood glue and screws. Test-fit the box over the window, and mark the wall for a 2x2 nailer or metal L-brackets for mounting the cornice. Fasten the nailer or brackets to the window header using screws.

Adding Molding. Finish the cornice by adding molding. Crown molding provides an attractive angled profile to the top, while base cap, panel cap, or small chair rail molding works well along the bottom. You can also install a flat bead molding (glass bead), so it covers the bottom edges of the box—a good option for a plywood box, which may have voids along the edges that would otherwise need filling.

Finish the cornice as desired; then mount it by screwing through the top piece into the nailer or through the L-brackets into the top piece.

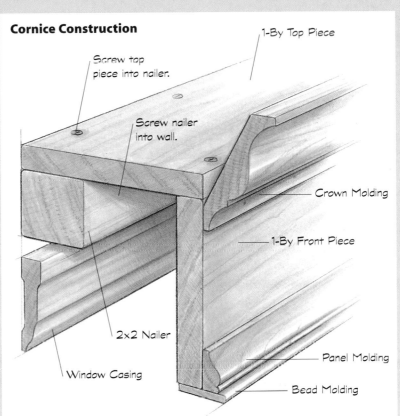

Cornice Construction

Screw top piece into nailer.

Screw nailer into wall.

1-By Top Piece

Crown Molding

1-By Front Piece

2×2 Nailer

Window Casing

Panel Molding

Bead Molding

Shutters

Due to the high cost and scarcity of glass, shutters were once used in place of windows in some areas of the country. In early Colonial homes, interior shutters were often used along with exterior shutters to close windowless openings against the elements and intruders. As high-quality glass windows became more commonplace, interior shutters became much more refined and decorative and were used primarily for privacy and controlling the flow of light. Today, shutters of all descriptions are added as much for decoration as they are for function. Whether their style is formal or rustic, shutters always add a touch of charm to a room's design. They have a clean, uncluttered appearance and a solidness when closed that adds a sense of security. Their precise lines and smooth finishes work well alone or provide a nice contrast to the soft textures of curtains.

CHOOSING A SHUTTER STYLE

Traditionally, shutters in historic homes had solid wood panels that completely covered the window when closed and often could be locked from the inside with iron bars. In finer interiors, shutters typically had raised-panel construction, following the styling of the surrounding wall paneling or other room elements. In rustic country homes, shutter doors were often made with simple plank-and-batten construction. Many traditional styles are still available today, but the most common style by far is the louvered-panel shutter.

Louvered Shutters. Louvered shutters are available with both fixed and adjustable louvers. Both types are good choices for interiors because they provide privacy and ventilation, but adjustable louvers make it easier to control the flow of light and air into a room. Installing multiple tiers of adjustable shutters over a single window adds even more versatility for controlling air and light. Louvered shutters are often labeled as either "traditional" (louvers that are up to 2 inches wide) or "plantation" (louvers that are 2 inches wide or more). While both types are well suited to most decorating styles, plantation shutters are generally considered contemporary in style.

Because shutters in early American homes had solid panels and were used for securing window openings, opposite, modern versions of the same can be especially appropriate for some traditional interiors.

Commonly used in more contemporary settings, above, plantation shutters have wide louvers that create bold shadow lines and have a somewhat more masculine look than traditional, finely louvered styles.

Louvered shutters, right, are a natural choice for enjoying the full benefits of entry-door sidelights. Here, the painted wood of the shutters fits well with the paneling and trimwork around the door.

Alternative Styles. Along with the standard types, specialty shutter manufacturers offer a fairly wide range of alternative panel styles. The arch-top, or "lazy arch," shutter is a popular decorative style used for arched windows or to add flair to square or rectangular windows. Shutter doors with fabric panels instead of louvers can include fabrics that coordinate with other patterns and colors in the room. Louvers can also be combined with solid panels for a more traditional look. Some solid-panel styles have decorative cutouts with motifs such as

hearts, moons, and stars, or with detailed open work.

Most shutters are hinged, either with multiple panels that unfold accordion-style or as single-panel types that are hinged only at the sides of the window. The latter is a typical style for plantation shutters. You can also find sliding shutters and complete shutter sets with integral sills. Shutters that cover only the lower portion of a window are called "cafe-style." This popular configuration offers privacy when the shutters are closed while still letting in light from the upper window area.

them so that they can be swung completely out of the window opening. Avoid single-panel shutters, especially plantation types that hang within a heavy box frame. These types block a lot of light even when the louver slats are open, and the large panels are so obtrusive when opened that most people keep them closed at all times.

Partial shutters, opposite, provide privacy and both filtered and direct sunlight.

Vertical louvers on the top tier combined with solid panels, left, add an unusual design touch.

Multilevel shutters, below, can help to de-emphasize the imposing scale and exposure of a tall window without blocking too much light.

OTHER CONSIDERATIONS

When open, shutters can either be concealed (as well as possible) or remain highly visible to serve as window decoration. Window frames in finer historic homes often had clever systems by which shutters slid sideways into wall pockets or folded into recesses (called shutter boxes) in the sides of deep window frames. Victorian homeowners hid shutters behind curtains and heavy drapery. If you desire less-visible shutters, choose a type that has small panels that can fold up against the sides of the window frame. The finish you apply will further define the shutters' role: when painted or stained to match walls or woodwork, shutters blend in with the decor for a subtle effect, while a contrasting finish makes shutters more noticeable.

One reason some people don't like shutters is that they block light. Even louvered shutters in fully open positions restrict a considerable amount of light, as what light comes through is mostly indirect. If you desire full light in the daytime, choose multipaneled shutters and install

BUYING & INSTALLING SHUTTERS

Building custom shutters from scratch is not a project many do-it-yourselfers are willing to undertake, but installing them is fairly simple. You can buy shutters in stock sizes at home centers and lumberyards, or you can order custom-fitted shutters from window shade retailers and shutter manufacturers. Better-quality and custom shutters come in a greater variety of styles and wood types (as well as vinyl) than stock products, but at a higher price.

With their smooth, washable surfaces and inherent charm, above, shutters are particularly well suited to kitchens. Louvered shutters in multiple levels allow you to make the most of morning sunlight without compromising privacy.

Plantation shutters, below, enhance the architectural appeal of this arch-top window, where curtains or drapes would mask it. Shutters also come in arch-top styles to match a window's shape.

SMART TIP | Painting Shutters

Painting shutters with a brush or paint pad is a time consuming task, because you must cover the front and back of each slat, the edges of the slats, and the edges of the frame. You can cut work time and achieve good results by spray painting the shutters. Work in a garage or outdoors on a windless day. Use drop cloths to protect against overspray.

Installing Stock Shutters

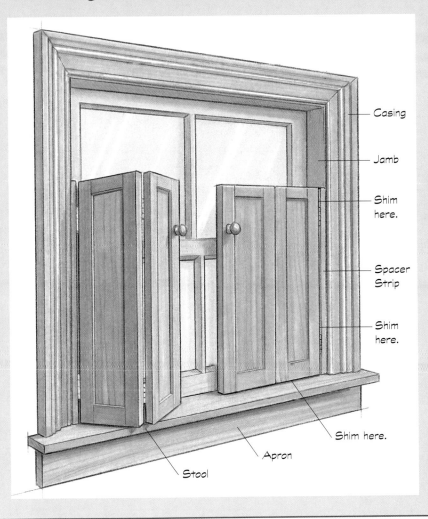

Casing

Jamb

Shim here.

Spacer Strip

Shim here.

Shim here.

Apron

Stool

To install multipanel stock shutters, tape the panels together and test-fit them in the opening, using shims (or coins) along the bottom to create a gap for swing clearance. Trim the shutters or spacer strips as needed, removing the same amount of material from each piece. Join the panels with nonmortise hinges; then add the mounting hinges to the outside panels, making sure all panels are perfectly aligned. (Some hinges have elongated holes for making minor adjustments.) After test-fitting again, remove the hinges and finish the shutters as desired. Finish and install the spacer blocks against the side jambs (for inside-mount shutters). Mount the shutters to the side jambs (or side casing) or spacer strips, using shims to set the proper gaps.

Stock shutters typically are wood or wood-composite, with individual panels in widths from 6 to 12 inches and heights from 20 to 48 inches If the measurements don't exactly fit your windows, you can trim the shutter panels or use wood spacer strips fastened to the window jambs. To simplify installation, use nonmortise hinges, which mount to the shutter surface without the need for mortised recesses.

Standard hinged (bifold) shutters can be installed on the inside of the window frame, against the side jambs; or on the outside of the frame, against the side casing. (See "Installing Stock Shutters," above.) Unless the shutters are custom-fit to your window, the outside mount-ing method is easier because it allows for some flexibility in shutter size and won't be affected by an out-of-square window. Many people like the inside mount because it presents a cleaner look as the shutter appears to be a part of the window.

Installation of custom shutters varies by manufacturer, so contact your dealer if you want to install your own custom shutters. To install stock shutters, choose a panel combination that is only slightly smaller or larger than your window opening, if not just the right size. Be sure to account for the thicknesses of all the hinges. If the shutters are smaller than the window, buy wood strips to use as spacers along the sides.

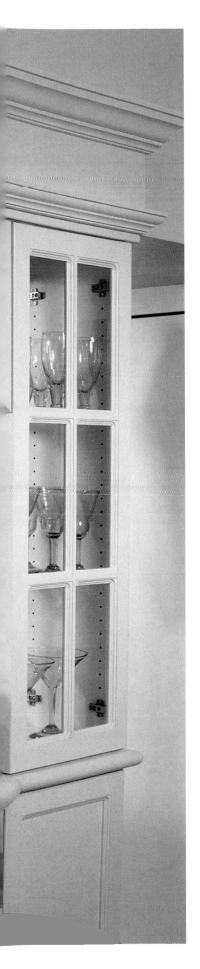

CHAPTER 5

TRIMMED WALL OPENINGS

*J*ust as doors and windows are portals to the outdoors, wall openings, pass-throughs, and passageways connect the interior spaces of your home. Wall openings allow travel and communication between rooms and promote the flow of light and air across what would otherwise be enclosed spaces. As architectural details, openings expand your views, functioning like interior windows to make rooms feel more spacious and dynamic. Because openings frame your view into the spaces beyond, improving the look of the opening also improves your perception of the adjoining spaces. In other situations, adding a pass-through or decorative opening in a solid wall can be just the right change for rooms that feel too confined or separated from other areas.

Pass-Throughs

As an opening in a wall, a pass-through visually joins two spaces, and it has the novel function of allowing items to be passed through a wall from one room to another. This feature makes pass-throughs especially useful in kitchen walls, but with a little creative planning, pass-throughs can be applied to great effect in other places in a home.

KITCHEN PASS-THROUGHS

A well-designed pass-through can greatly improve the atmosphere of a kitchen as well as the way it works. From a functional standpoint, a pass-through enables cooks to hand plates and food into an adjacent dining area without leaving the kitchen. This basic convenience is what led to the creation of the pass-through and is the reason why kitchen pass-throughs in old homes tended to be small and often included a door to seal off the space.

Today, pass-throughs provide much more than convenience. They bring light into kitchens and allow cooks to be a part of the activity in other rooms while keeping the

kitchen partially enclosed to contain noise and cooking odors. When the wall is opened up in front of a primary work area, such as the sink, range, or main prep counter, the cook can enjoy expanded views and communication with others while remaining in the kitchen.

Pass-Through Shelves. One of the best features of a pass-through is the shelf or countertop space at the bottom of the opening. Kitchen pass-throughs typically include a small countertop that matches the main one in the kitchen.

Raised shelves tend to be used more as decorative surfaces than as work areas. The height separation means that the surface is protected from water and countertop messes, making it a good surface for storing everyday items, such as the mail. The raised ledge also blocks the view of dirty dishes from other rooms. When the countertop runs flush into the pass-through, there is no visual barrier as with the ledge, and the extra countertop creates more usable work space. Extending the countertop beyond the opening into the other room turns the pass-through into a breakfast bar.

HALLWAYS & LIVING AREAS

In other areas of the home, pass-throughs can provide strong links between spaces without joining them entirely. For example, in older homes many rooms are almost completely enclosed units connected by hallways. Adding a pass-through between a hallway and a common area, such as a library or living room, makes the room feel more spacious and the hallway feel less tunnel-like.

A great way to make the most of a hallway pass-through is to hang artwork (or photographs or wall hangings) on the far hallway wall so that it can be viewed from the adjacent room. Position the artwork so that the pass-through acts as a large frame that showcases the artwork from the room-side perspective.

Before a sunroom was added to the back of the house, the pass-through shown opposite bottom was a window. Now the addition can be enjoyed from the kitchen as well.

The creative design of this pass-through, left, includes a notched arch at the top and a wooden shelf with apron trim at the bottom. Its display of decorative items suggests that the opening is used more for light and communication than for passing plates.

Kitchens are public places where most people spend a lot of their time. Imagine what a cook in the kitchen below would be missing if this pass-through were a solid wall.

DESIGNING A PASS-THROUGH

Designing and building a pass-through is not a difficult project. The construction involved is fairly simple, providing the wall is a partition wall and not load-bearing. Openings in load-bearing walls require a structural beam that spans the opening and supports the load above—a job for a contractor. You can finish a new pass-through or add trim to an existing one in a variety of ways. One popular treatment is to wrap the inside of the opening with jambs of finish lumber, then install casing on both sides, in the manner of a window surround. The illustration on the next page shows what's involved.

Countertop Pass-Throughs. Countertops for pass-throughs can be ordered custom-made from a countertop manufacturer. The materials are the same as for kitchen countertops: plastic laminate, solid-surface, stainless steel,

and other fabricated materials. An economical option is to cut your own laminate top using a blank bought from a home center and finish the edges with iron-on laminate strips. To create your own tiled countertop, first build a shelf base with two pieces of plywood topped with a layer of cement-based backerboard. Lay the tile over the backerboard using thin-set mortar, and the surface should last forever. For pass-throughs in rooms other than kitchens, a finished wood shelf may be more appropriate.

When planning the location and size of the pass-through, think about how much visibility you want to have from both sides of the opening. For example, you might not want a full view of a messy kitchen while you're eating in the dining room, or to create a sight line from the entryway into a more private space. Adding doors or shutters to enclose the pass-through easily solves these problems, however, and they add a decorative feature to the opening.

A little decorative opening, above, with a door provides an interesting view between an entryway and living room. It's arched top playfully mimics the grand windows of the main room.

A secluded and often neglected place in many homes, the dining room, below, stays well connected by means of multiple wall openings. Heavy trimwork helps the unconventional openings remain in keeping with the room's traditional decor.

DECOR TIP | Folding Shutters

Folding, louvered shutters can be easily installed to the sides of a pass-through. They can cover all of the opening or just the lower portion for a cafe-style treatment.

Creating a Pass-Through

Once you've made sure the wall is not load-bearing and have checked for utilities, such as pipes, wires, and ductwork, cut out the opening to the desired size. A pass-through has a simple 2x4 frame, with a horizontal sill and header attached to studs at either side of the opening. Add cripple studs for support and to provide backing for attaching the drywall.

If possible, use existing studs for one or both sides of the frame. Add studs as needed; then install the sill and header, making sure the frame is square.

Patch the drywall (or other surface material) as needed. For an untrimmed opening, cover the inside of the framing with drywall; then add corner bead and finish the edges. For a wood-trim application, add one-by finish-grade jambs inside the opening, and install casing on both sides of the wall.

To add a shelf, notch the ends of the shelf to create horns that will receive the bottom ends of the side casing, and add an apron board below the shelf in the style of a stool-and-apron window surround.

Pass-Through Construction

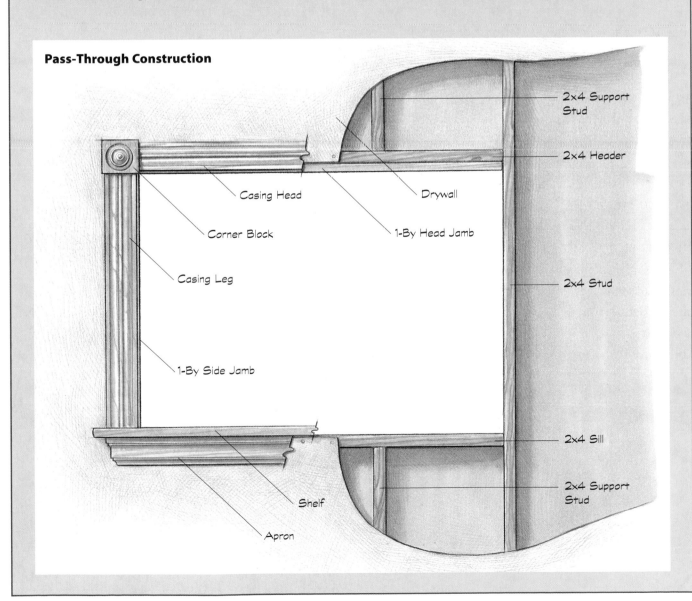

- 2x4 Support Stud
- 2x4 Header
- Casing Head
- Drywall
- Corner Block
- 1-By Head Jamb
- Casing Leg
- 2x4 Stud
- 1-By Side Jamb
- 2x4 Sill
- 2x4 Support Stud
- Shelf
- Apron

Passageways

Passageways enable you to walk from room to room, but they also have an impact on how well your home works. A well-defined passageway clearly divides areas and allows for a change in decor, while a more subtle room transition demands greater continuity of style between living spaces. A passageway can also affect the feel of a room. For example, a living room has a more formal feel if there is a decorated entrance through which to walk.

Archways look great with many decorating styles, below. Pilasters add a classical touch to an eclectic scheme, while the broad arch contributes to a range of curvilinear forms.

Although massive, the columns and header shown opposite give this high-ceilinged room a human scale. Without the passageway, the space would feel too large for comfort.

TRIM TIP | Quick Changes

Adding molding to a nondescript passageway provides a dramatic improvement. Another option calls for installing brackets, such as the one shown here, to embellish a passageway.

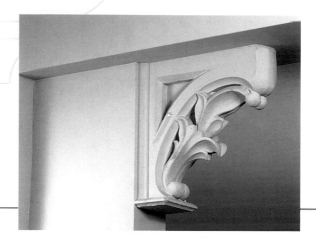

TRADITIONAL PASSAGEWAYS

Like doorways and windows, interior passageways in historic homes were important architectural elements. Georgian rooms were entered through tall, often deep, passageways with semicircular arched tops. Characteristically, Federal entryways were broad, with columns or pilasters at the sides supporting an elegant, elliptical arch.

To subdivide their open floor plans, Craftsman homes included beautiful wood room dividers, typically with low bookcases or cabinets extending from the walls at either side and topped with short, square columns reaching up to a trimmed soffit or ceiling beam. Before drywall became the building standard, homes with plaster walls often included arched passageways.

REDEFINING OPENINGS

In contrast to the decorative, often ornate passageways in older homes, today's home designs typically treat passageways minimally, with room transitions sometimes defined only by a change in flooring or ceiling texture. But adding some definition and architectural detail to a passageway is easy, because the structural opening already exists.

The plain passageways common in modern homes often consist of nothing more than short wing walls defining the sides of the opening. One simple but effective change you can make to these is to install a false header, or soffit, to bring down the ceiling and add dimension to the top of the opening. To complete the transformation, wrap the entire opening with wood jambs, and trim the sides and header with decorative molding. (See "Dressing Up a Passageway," on page 85.)

Archway Kits. For a different effect, you can turn a square-cornered passage into an archway using a couple of different methods. One method is to use a do-it-yourself archway trim kit. Archway trim kits are available from

SMART TIP | Drywall Arches

If you're adding an archway during new construction, cover the curve of the arch with ¼-inch drywall cut to fit. Begin fastening at the top of the arch, and work your way down. Finish the edges with a flexible corner bead for a neat appearance.

architectural products dealers and generally come in a few different neoclassical styles. Made of MDF and paint-grade solid wood, complete kits include an arch top (with a C-shape design made to fit over a drywalled soffit) and two columns or pilaster assemblies for the sides of the opening. Arches are also available individually.

Installation. To install a kit, remove any trim from the existing opening; add blocking and triangular drywall pieces at the top corners; then fit and attach the arch and columns. The kit pieces are available in a variety of sizes, and you can custom-order pieces to fit nonstandard wall thicknesses. If your passageway is open all the way to the ceiling, you'll need to add a false header before installing the archway kit. (See "Dressing up a Passageway," page 85.) Another way to create an arched passageway is to use prefabricated arch corners that you install directly over wood or steel framing. The 4½-inch-thick material of the corners butts flush against standard drywall and requires no finishing along the curved edges.

An arched overlook, opposite, opens up a closed-in staircase and the hallway beyond.

A salvaged door pediment, above, gives this plain passageway a sense of architectural heritage. Originally an exterior detail, the piece was left unfinished by the new owner to show its age.

Carved wood grilles, right, were popular doorway embellishments in Victorian homes. The custom of the time was to hang heavy curtains (portieres) from a rod below the grille, although the beautiful fretwork alone seems more appropriate for a modern setting.

5

TRIMMED WALL OPENINGS

Other Options. Further along the spectrum lies a number of variations on the standard passageway. Columns are a natural choice and have been used for this purpose for centuries. (See Chapter 10 for a discussion of columns and the column-and-pedestal room divider.) Other ideas include screens, curtains, glass panels, hanging beads—in short, anything that signifies a threshold or serves as a partial barrier of some kind. Salvaged items are also great options: architectural elements such as door lintels, wooden arches, ironwork, corbels, and brackets can be incorporated into a built-in passageway.

When pulled aside, the fabric walls at right become sensual decorative passageways. In homes with modest square footage, a full view across adjoining spaces (especially a diagonal view) creates the illusion of a larger floor plan.

Passageways with large double doors, below, can be just as welcoming as they are private. Glazed bifold doors bring light into this sitting room but separate it from the house entrance.

Dressing Up a Passageway

If you have plain passageway with no transition at the ceiling, add a false header above the opening. Build the header with 2x4 lumber, creating a ladder-like frame with a top and bottom plate running the full width of the opening; add studs on the ends and every 16 inches in between. Attach the header to the wall studs and ceiling joists, using screws. Cover the sides of the frame with drywall, so the header is flush with the side walls of the opening.

Finish the Opening. Install flat jambs inside the opening, making sure the outside edges of the boards are flush with both sides of the walls and header. You can add any type of casing and header detail to cover the jamb edges, but make sure to leave a reveal as is done with door and window casings. The trim surround shown here follows traditional styling and includes fluted side casings and a header assembly made up of built-up molding profiles.

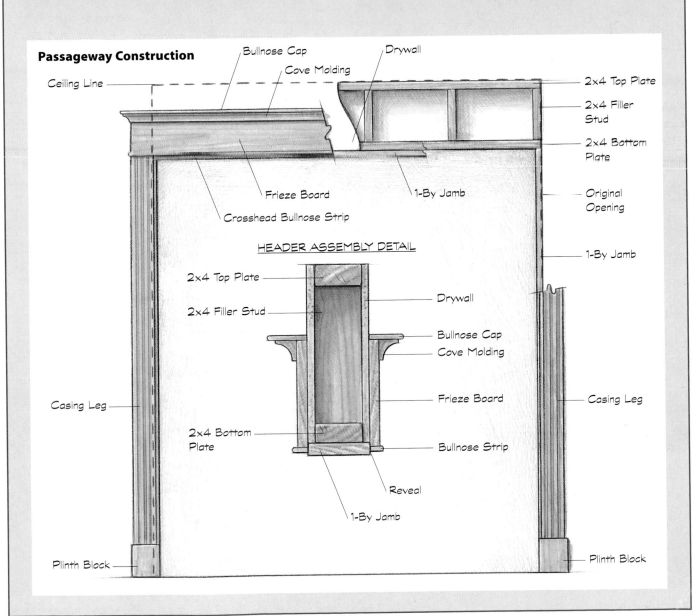

Passageway Construction

Bullnose Cap
Cove Molding
Drywall
Ceiling Line
2x4 Top Plate
2x4 Filler Stud
2x4 Bottom Plate
1-By Jamb
Original Opening
Frieze Board
Crosshead Bullnose Strip
1-By Jamb

HEADER ASSEMBLY DETAIL

2x4 Top Plate
2x4 Filler Stud
Drywall
Bullnose Cap
Cove Molding
Casing Leg
Frieze Board
Casing Leg
2x4 Bottom Plate
Bullnose Strip
Reveal
1-By Jamb
Plinth Block
Plinth Block

Decorative Wall Openings

Wall openings intended neither as pass-throughs nor passageways can be purely decorative or, depending on their size and placement, can play important functional roles in your home. As "windows" in interior walls, openings can let light and air into confined spaces, connect rooms with one another, and create interesting views, or they simply can be used as architectural features to break up large expanses of blank walls.

Appearing in homes in various forms more or less randomly throughout history, wall openings are not representative of any one period style—and that makes them fun to design. Thomas Jefferson added them to his Monticello home just as Japanese builders carved them into walls of teahouses.

BUILDING A WALL OPENING

Creating a new wall opening is similar to adding a pass-through. (See "Creating a Pass-Through," on page 79.) The project is much simpler in non-load-bearing (partition) walls, which are not part of the house's supporting structure. Once you cut away the wall surface and any interfering studs, you can build a frame for the opening in almost any size or shape. In load-bearing walls, you can make narrow openings by cutting away the drywall between wall studs. This will yield a maximum opening width of 14½ inches before adding any finishes or trim.

DECORATING IDEAS

Incorporating the opening into the existing room decor is merely a matter of choosing the right trimwork. You can match the casing of the regular windows for an echo

The fanlight, opposite, was a classic detail of the Federal style and has remained popular ever since. Unique lead work for each of these lights lends a distinct character to the rooms they preside over.

Openings located high on a wall, left, allow spaces to share light but help maintain privacy in both rooms.

A sliding paneled door and hand-stenciled trim, above, give this little opening a lot of charm. To add a similar door to a wall opening, enlarge the opening to create a pocket inside the wall. Doors like this can move either horizontally or vertically.

effect. Finish round openings on the inside with flexible drywall and molding. A shelf at the bottom of an opening makes it an interesting display space, like a niche that can be viewed from both sides of the wall. You can simply paint a wood shelf, or if the opening is in a kitchen wall, install a countertop material that matches the kitchen counters. Shutters or stained-glass panels reinforce the interior window theme and provide privacy when needed. If you want to bring light into a space but still need privacy and sound control, fill the opening with glass block or frames of textured glass. A visit to an architectural salvage yard might yield some good ideas—an old window sash or a grille of decorative ironwork could make a striking detail when set into a wall opening.

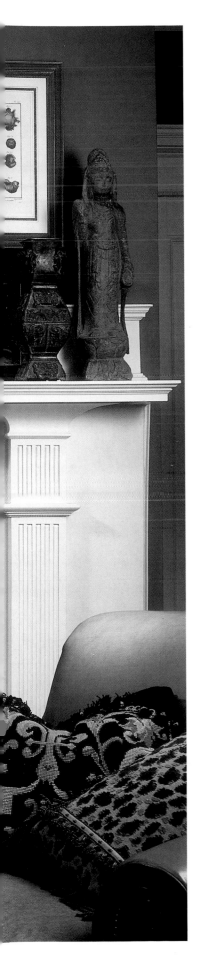

CHAPTER 6

FIREPLACE MANTELS

*T*he fireplace has evolved from an open hearth in the middle of the floor to the various types of masonry enclosures we know today. But it wasn't until the advent of the decorative mantel that the fireplace earned its dominant role in interior architecture. The term "mantel" refers to the entire decorative surround and not just the shelf. In historic homes, the quality of a mantel indicated the homeowner's status, and its form was a showpiece for the architect's personal art and the handiwork of many local craftsmen. Today, it remains as the social and aesthetic focus of any room it occupies. Replacing an old, skimpy mantel or embellishing a bland brick surround not only transforms the appearance of your fireplace, it can change the architecture of the entire room.

Anatomy of a Mantel

The classic decorative mantel was a product of the Italian Renaissance, and its basic structure is still used today. A mantel includes four main parts: the field, the pilasters or columns, the mantelshelf, and the decorative molding. Some mantels also include an overmantel—a decorative treatment applied to the wall above the mantelshelf, often intended to receive a framed picture or painting.

The field is the inverted "U" frame of the mantel, made up of two vertical side boards and a horizontal frieze board. It is the foundation to which the other mantel parts are attached. With a traditional masonry fireplace, the field covers a portion of the brick opening and overlaps onto the surrounding wall surface. The band of brick left exposed is called the slip; it is often kept plain or decorated with a noncombustible finish, such as ceramic tile, marble, or metal.

Columns and Shelf. Standing at each side of the opening, a pilaster or column adds a sense of structure to the mantel and visually carries the mantelshelf above. In the classical mode, pilasters and columns may be mounted atop plinth blocks or bases and crowned with a capital or block. The mantelshelf traditionally is a solid piece of wood measuring 1 to 2 inches in thickness, with a milled front edge or molding added for a decorative profile. Support for the shelf can come from molding, blocks above pilasters or columns, brackets, or any kind of decorative projection centered along the frieze.

Marble mantels, left, are popular in traditional-style homes. Although wood is the most popular material, stone, tile, and even solid surfacing are used on mantels.

While less common than pilasters, a nearly full-radius column, below, provides a deep projection to the mantel's profile and adds a strong visual feature.

Mantel Anatomy

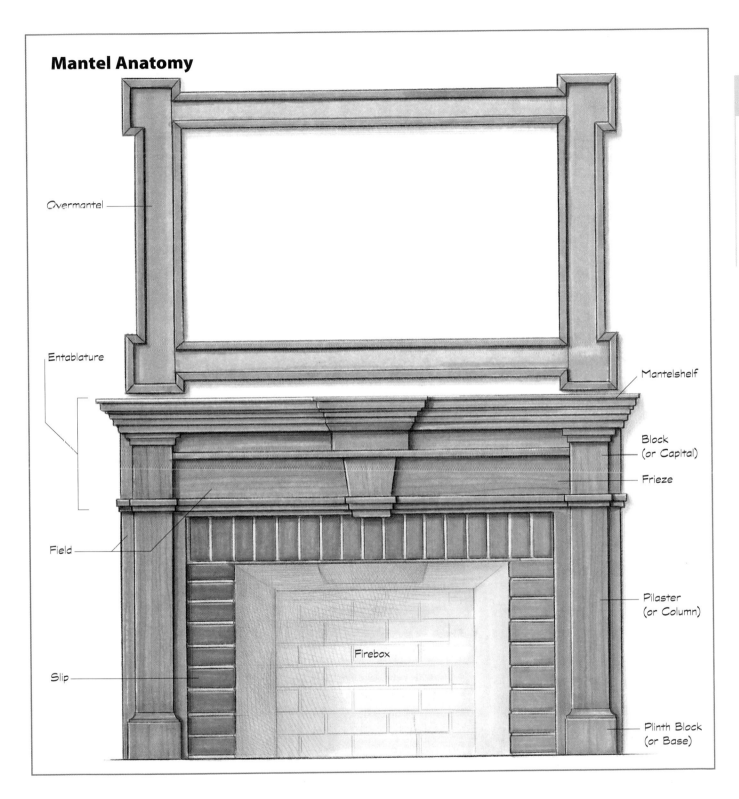

Overmantel

Entablature

Mantelshelf

Block (or Capital)

Frieze

Field

Pilaster (or Column)

Slip

Firebox

Plinth Block (or Base)

6

FIREPLACE MANTELS

Mantel Moldings. Molding finishes the mantel. As with a built-up cornice, a combination of relatively simple trim pieces can add up to a deceptively complex treatment. Cove, bead, half-round, crown molding, or a simple astragal band or carved frieze trim are used to add rich detail to the mantel while cleverly hiding gaps, fasteners, and joints.

In addition to trimwork, friezes and blocks are often adorned with carved wooden plaques and appliqués.

While most mantels are made of wood, marble, stone, brick, river rock, iron, copper, and plaster were also commonly used for historical mantels. Modern mantels can include concrete, glass, cast-stone, stucco, and polymers.

Period Mantels

As powerful symbols of domestic life, mantels have received special attention by designers throughout history and remain as some of the best examples of the major architectural periods.

Colonial Mantels. Decorative mantels weren't common in American homes until later in the Colonial period because the early settlers did little to beautify their large, utilitarian fireplaces. As the colonies developed and homes became more refined, mantels appeared in simple forms of wooden trimwork surrounding coarse brick openings. Some versions had a narrow mantelshelf. In the eighteenth century, fireplace openings were often surrounded by wood paneling that extended over the entire fireplace wall.

Georgian Mantels. The grand homes of the Georgian period featured the mantel as an important showpiece of bold, classical styling. Large pilasters led up to a carved or molded mantelshelf, which was not deep but often quite high. An overmantel was very common and often included a rectangular frame and a second set of pilasters or columns supporting a broken pediment above. The mantel detailing frequently tied into the room's ceiling cornice. Moldings carried deep profiles of classical design: egg-and-dart, acanthus leaf, key, and dentil motifs.

Federal Mantels. The restrained classical detailing of the Federal period created exceptionally elegant mantels. Their basic form and proportions have become a standard for much of traditional mantel design. Evolving out of the Georgian model and influenced heavily by the decorative designs of the English Adam style, Federal mantels included the basic parts in refined forms and typically had no overmantel. Frieze panels decorated with garlands, urns, and carved appliqués are characteristic features, as are delicate moldings of classical motifs and the use of built-up molding treatments.

Colonial fireplace mantels, below left, were of plain design and usually integrated into the surrounding room decor.

A richly decorated overmantel, below, with broken pediment was a key characteristic of Georgian fireplaces.

Victorian Mantels. Victorian mantel design is characterized most markedly by its break with classical rules of composition. While many versions employed classical elements, such as pilasters, columns, entablatures, and classical moldings, these were mixed liberally with Gothic shapes, spindle work, and Asian and other "exotic" imagery. Typical examples have ornate, imaginative designs and often include overmantels with display shelves and inset mirrors.

Craftsman Mantels. Craftsman-style mantels are simple and organic, relying on the natural beauty of raw materials rather than formal ornamentation. The classic wood frame facing of previous styles is replaced by flat fields of brick or tile, the latter usually with a monochrome, earth-tone finish or storied pattern. Many examples include a heavy wood mantelshelf with simple brackets or modillion blocks for support, often with a recessed nook above for displaying decorative items. Use of molding, if any, is minimal. A novel feature of the Craftsman style is the fireplace inglenook—an alcove housing the fireplace in the center with bench seating on either side.

Narrow frieze panels, above, with delicate swags and finely carved plaques are sure signs of Federal-style mantels.

This ornate Victorian mantel, below left, shows a creative mix of elements typical of the period. Tall pilasters have a classical look but with unconventional, organic top ends. Dentil molding supports a cornice at the top of the overmantel but stops short in a decidedly nonclassical fashion.

The mantel in this Craftsman-inspired interior, below, has a brick facing with an organic texture and medieval arch motif over the fireplace opening. The fine yet plain mantelshelf is consistent with the room's trimwork.

Designing Your Mantel

There are no strict guidelines for mantel design, but traditional wooden mantels tend to follow a few basic design criteria. The one specification that you must include is proper clearance between the fireplace opening and any combustible parts of the mantel.

Most fire-safety codes require 6 inches of clearance to combustible materials that project up to ¾ inch from the face of the fireplace, and 12 inches of clearance to projections equal to or greater than 1½ inches. Other design considerations are based on the type of fireplace you have, the mantel's style, and whether it will be custom-built or ordered as a kit.

Classical architecture receives a modern interpretation in the elegant mantel design shown left. Streamlined pilaster forms intersect a simple crown molding below the mantelshelf. A fine band of molding subtly creates the look of an entablature.

The combustible parts of a mantel, above, should be placed at least 6 in. from the firebox opening.

This elaborate yet refined mantel, opposite, employs Georgian-style features to enhance a projecting fireplace wall: a surround full of classical detailing, an overmantel framing a decorative mirror, and fluted pilasters starting at a paneled wainscot and extending up to the ceiling cornice.

TRADITIONAL DESIGNS

For a traditional wooden mantel, a good model with which to start is the basic four-part type shown in "Mantel Anatomy," page 91. This style of mantel has a field with vertical side boards that are 7 to 13 inches wide. The frieze board of the field should be between 1 and 2 times as wide as the side boards—enough room for the moldings and a flat area below for additional decoration. The mantelshelf may be anywhere from 5 to 12 inches deep, but it should fit the proportions of the mantel overall and not overhang its supporting moldings by more than a few inches.

SMART TIP | Fireplace Care

If your fireplace has never worked properly, have it checked by a professional before you start the cosmetic work. Sometimes a poor draw can be remedied by something as simple as adding a layer of bricks that raises the firebox floor.

COLUMNS & PILASTERS

Pilasters or columns extend from the floor to the underside of the shelf and are narrower than the vertical field boards, even with molding applied. The middle sections of pilasters can be fluted, reeded, recess-paneled, or left plain, while columns look especially ornate when wrapped with vines or floral strands. Plinths and bases add architectural weight to pilasters and columns, as do top blocks and capitals. Square-edged plinths and blocks also serve as projections for wrapping with molding. Frieze panels can receive almost any type of decoration, but traditional styling always calls for symmetry and balance. A central block helps break up the frieze and can project for additional molding detail.

Mantelshelves. Most mantelshelves are between 52 and 62 inches above the floor, although this varies based on the size of the fireplace and whether the hearth is raised or flush with the floor. For best appearance, the sides of the mantel should be aligned with or extend just beyond the sides of a flush hearth; for a raised hearth, the mantel should equal the hearth width or be slightly narrower.

If you're adding tile to the slips around the fireplace opening, choose a tile size that will result in a minimum of cuts. Above the opening, start with a full tile in the center rather than a grout joint, and place any cut tiles along the side slips at the bottom. Cover the outside edges of the tile with a small molding, or mill a rabbet into the field boards to receive the tile edges.

A massive stone mantel, opposite, epitomizes the decorating term "anchor." The Gothic arch and projecting lion mask are medieval features.

This simple wooden mantel, below, features a clever departure from conventional design.

A cabin-style setting would be incomplete without a rustic fireplace, above right. The craftsman who built this custom mantel added a secondary mantelshelf for decorative items.

Before central heating systems, all rooms were heated by fireplaces, right. Those in bedrooms and other private areas were smaller and decorated more simply than fireplaces in public rooms.

Building Your Own Mantel

The best thing about building a mantel is that you can construct almost all of it in your workshop, then install it as one piece. A few power tools that will make the job go smoothly are a biscuit joiner for assembling the field boards, a power miter saw for making all the miter cuts on the trim molding, and a pneumatic finish nailer for attaching the molding.

There are a number of places to find mantel designs, including woodworking books and magazines. Another option is to find a mantel you like and duplicate its design. Sketch the overall design on graph paper; then break down the design into individual components. You can reproduce most wooden mantels with standard molding profiles. After removing your old mantel, take measurements and make a scaled drawing of the new mantel from which to work. If you're adding tile, select the tile before building the mantel to be sure the dimensions are correct.

Installing the Mantel. Center the mantel over the fireplace opening, and fasten it to the wall studs with screws or 16d casing nails. Countersink the fasteners and plug or putty the holes. Add thin edge molding along the outside edges of the field boards and along the tile or brick inside the field. If necessary, plane or trim the molding to follow wall contours. Also add molding along the back edge of the shelf if there are any large gaps.

The handsome Federal-style mantel shown above may seem impossible to duplicate, but you can come fairly close by using standard materials. In addition to using moldings for the mantel, install marble tiles on the slip area.

Careful planning has greatly improved the look of this simple fireplace, right. Two rows of tile visually extend the hearth up to the bottom of firebox, while two more rows cover the black metal case along the top. A traditional wooden surround adds an attractive frame and a built-in appearance.

Mantel Construction

The illustration below shows a basic four-piece mantel made with ¾-inch MDF, which is a good choice for a mantel you'll be painting. The shelf is made from two layers of MDF laminated together with glue and screws. If you prefer a natural-grain finish, use a finish-grade plywood with a hardwood veneer and cover all of the exposed edges with molding.

The Main Pieces. To build the mantel, cut the side field boards and frieze board, and join them with biscuits and glue. Assemble the shelf, and attach it to the top edges of the field with glue and screws, mak-

ing sure it is perpendicular to the field. Attach the pilasters and any blocks at the ends by screwing through the back of the field. Install an entablature block the same way.

Molding Applications. You can add molding that won't come in contact with the wall or fireplace opening while the mantel is still on your bench. Install other molding to hide gaps after you have mounted the mantel to the wall. However, you might choose to hide the mounting fasteners behind some molding, and therefore would leave off the appropriate pieces until later.

Mantel Construction

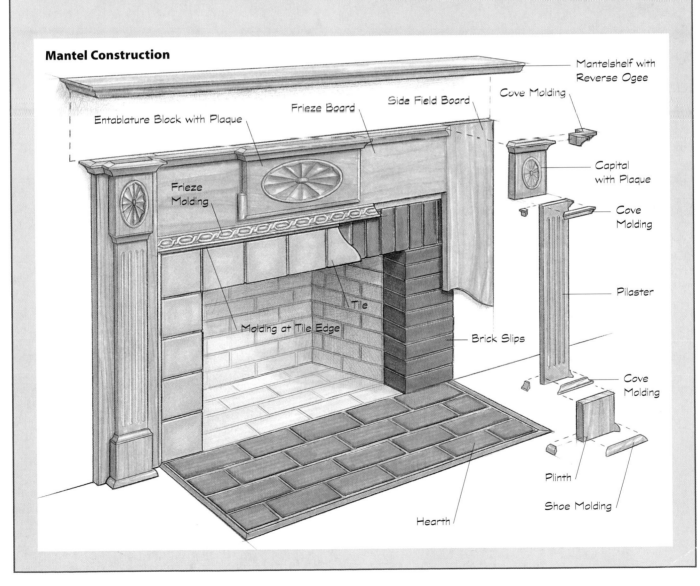

Mantelshelf with Reverse Ogee

Entablature Block with Plaque

Frieze Board

Side Field Board

Cove Molding

Capital with Plaque

Frieze Molding

Cove Molding

Pilaster

Tile

Molding at Tile Edge

Brick Slips

Cove Molding

Plinth

Shoe Molding

Hearth

Mantel Kits

Install-it-yourself mantel kits are a great option for those who don't want to build a custom mantel. Complete mantels are available in wood, cast-stone, iron, plaster, and other materials. You can also order elements a la carte, such as overmantel decorations, columns and pilasters, mantelshelves, corbels and brackets, decorative blocks, and appliqués. Most manufacturers offer mantels in various traditional and contemporary styles in a few different materials and sizes, or you can order custom sizes and designs for an extra fee.

Kit Installation. Kit mantels are typically shipped in three pieces, plus trim and accessories. Assembly and installation are simple: attach the side pieces to the mantelshelf; install a mounting board to the wall; then fasten the shelf to the mounting board and the sidepieces to the wall. If you plan to paint the mantel, choose a model made of MDF, pine, or poplar, which are less expensive than hardwood versions. You can buy mantel kits through fireplace retail stores or through manufacturers' catalogs or Web sites.

Mantel Makeovers

Sprucing up an old fireplace might involve as little as changing the paint color or as much as remodeling the entire fireplace wall. Budgets vary, of course, but there are a lot of materials and design possibilities with which to work, for both do-it-yourself and professional projects.

If you've updated the rest of your house and the fireplace looks a little neglected and out of touch, paint the mantel to match the surrounding decor. For a slightly more invasive approach, update the mantel's trimwork or replace it altogether. To help generate decorating ideas, look to other design elements in your home. Some architects of the past liked to mimic exterior details in their mantel designs. In a modern home, a clever carpenter might use leftover railing stock from the home's main staircase to create custom molding under a mantelshelf.

In addition to classic rectangular forms, mantel kits are available in styles that break with traditional standards, opposite top. The curvilinear detailing and splayed pilasters of this kit mantel bring a touch of eighteenth-century France to a modern room.

Victorian mantels, with their rich wood hues and charming decoration, opposite bottom, are the epitome of domestic comfort. This relatively plain example bears an overmantel mirror and patterned-tile slips that are typical period features.

With a four-sided surround and continuous metal frame, above, this bedroom fireplace assumes the aspect of a wall hanging. The position of the fireplace allows it to be viewed from the bed.

Heavy curved molding, right, serves as a strong border for this tiled mantel. The mantel, framed print, and matching wall sconces create an appealing composition.

Hand-painted tiles, left, add a personal touch to fireplace slips. You can buy professionally made tiles at tile stores or through art dealers, or do it yourself at a paint-your-own pottery studio.

Veneer-stone, below, creates the look of traditional mortared stone at a fraction of the cost of real masonry. Special corner pieces effectively replicate the depth of actual stones.

Adding built-in bookcases and cabinets, opposite top, is an excellent way to fill the recesses that often flank a traditional fireplace.

The overmantel, opposite bottom, is often forgotten in modern designs. Here, a simple framed mirror makes an elegant design statement.

Adding Tile. Adding tile is one of the best ways to make over an old brick surround. Because tile is non-combustible, you can install it right up to the fireplace opening. A complete tile treatment might include covering a raised brick hearth or extending a flush hearth to cover a larger floor area. A flush mantel treatment with a tile field surrounding the fireplace opening and no shelf above has a clean, contemporary feel. Newer homes with original gas fireplaces often have a simple tile decoration and perhaps a small hearth. Remodeling these is relatively easy—you can replace the old tile with a more appealing style, add some bold trimwork for greater definition, or change the look entirely by installing a traditional wooden mantel with narrow slips of tile around the opening.

SMART TIP   Taking the Heat

When adding tile to a mantel surround, use a heat-resistant thinset and mortar. Standard thinset, organic mastics, and standard mortar can crack under extremely hot temperatures.

Stone Mantels. At the other end of the spectrum from molded wood and decorative tile surrounds is the cabin-style warmth of a mortared stone fireplace. By using veneer-stone, you can create the look of a real stone fireplace without even calling a mason. Veneer-stone is a molded cement product with natural pigments that convincingly imitates the appearance and texture of natural stone. Individual "stones" have flat back surfaces that install easily over the wall and a layer of metal mesh. The pieces are mortared into place in a random arrangement; then the spaces in between are filled with mortar and tooled. The most authentic-looking stone treatments include a projecting fireplace with veneer-stone running all the way up to the ceiling, imitating a stone chimney.

A fireplace remodel offers a good opportunity to add details to the fireplace wall. Built-in bookcases or cabinets set into recesses made by a projecting fireplace are a typical embellishment. When there's no space to the sides, you can add shallow bookcases or shelves to create a recess for the fireplace itself.

Zero-Clearance Fireplaces

Before the advent of zero-clearance fireplaces, homes that were built without hearths stayed that way. Adding a new masonry fireplace simply is not an option for most homeowners. But today's gas- and wood-burning zero-clearance units are so simple to install that they've become a viable option for even minor remodeling projects. Made of metal with a masonry lining, these self-contained fireplaces are lightweight enough to sit on a standard framed floor and can be surrounded by a wooden frame to within ½ inch of the main box (hence the name). A two-piece vent pipe draws outside air into the unit for combustion while exhausting smoke out of the house.

One clear drawback of zero-clearance fireplaces is that without the right decoration, they can look conspicuously artificial. Here are a few ideas that can help make one of these modern wonders look like a real masonry fireplace:

- Choose a model with a minimum of brass or other decorative metal features on the front panels.

- Cover the front of the box with ceramic tile; then surround the tile with a traditional mantel.

- Recess the unit into the floor so that the bottom of the firebox is flush with the floor surface, or build a raised hearth that is flush with the firebox. (Check with the manufacturer to make that sure the installation is safe for your model.)

Zero-clearance units, top, open up a number of design possibilities. This contemporary treatment does away with the traditional mantel.

A contemporary flush tile treatment, center, adds plenty of life to this fireplace without being obtrusive.

The stone surround and raised hearth, left, complement the design of this rustic-style room. The built-in wood box is a useful accessory.

Zero-Clearance Fireplace Installation

Zero-clearance units are great choices for remodeling projects. They are light enough for standard floor framing, and they can be installed within inches of drywall-covered walls. But their biggest advantage is the fact that there is often no need for a standard chimney or flue. With direct-vent units, the flue can exit the top, back, or sides of the firebox. That means you can install a unit against a wall and have the flue go through the wall directly to the outdoors. This opens up your design options. For example, with a direct-vent fireplace it is possible to install a unit under a window.

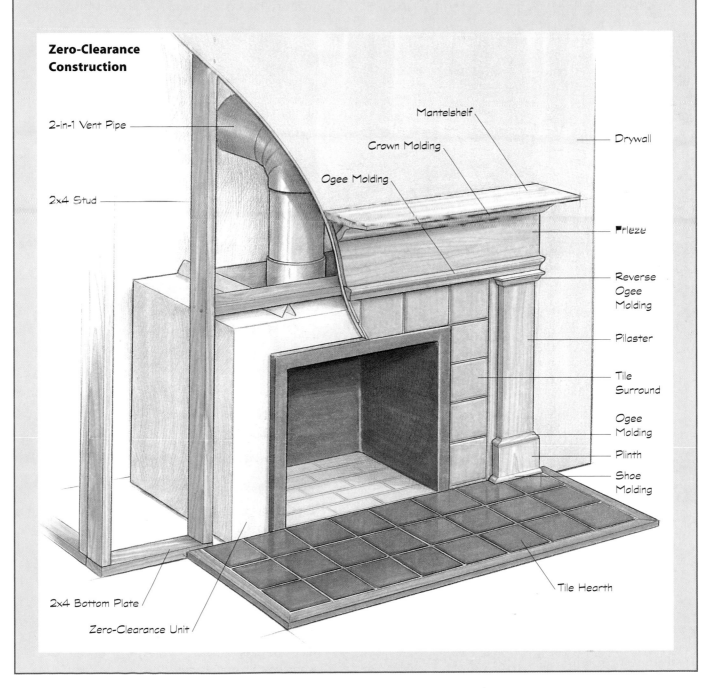

Zero-Clearance Construction

2-in-1 Vent Pipe

2x4 Stud

2x4 Bottom Plate

Zero-Clearance Unit

Mantelshelf

Crown Molding

Ogee Molding

Drywall

Frieze

Reverse Ogee Molding

Pilaster

Tile Surround

Ogee Molding

Plinth

Shoe Molding

Tile Hearth

Hortus Eystettensis. Eichstätt. 1613

CHAPTER 7

RECESSED NOOKS & DECORATIVE SHELVES

*D*ecorative nooks and shelves not only bring architectural interest to a wall, they also display a home's most personal items. As room elements and adornments, they are natural focal points that invite guests to ask questions about a particular piece or a fine collection. The most formal of these display features is the niche, the miniature, half-domed alcove found in churches and grand homes alike. Niches lend an illusory sense of depth to a wall while adding a touch of historical elegance. Recessed like a niche but less defined in style and form, the decorative nook has many uses and decorative functions. And decorative shelves, either wall-hung or built-in, are fundamental decorating tools that bring individuality to a design scheme.

Niches

The niche is a unique architectural detail with some interesting qualities. Its name derives from a French word meaning "to nest," a definition that captures the niche's aspect of a cradle or sacred place. With its arched shape and half-domed shell, the niche is also suggestive of a shrine, a symbolic temple, much like the miniature household shrines found in Eastern cultures. Indeed, niches are found in churches and sacred buildings of many religions, where they display statuary and various other objects of worship.

Of course, the niche is equally appropriate for secular settings and has been a popular interior ornament since ancient times. Gothic architecture favored the ecclesiastical use of niches, while classical interiors employed them more as striking displays for busts, urns, or vases. The

DECOR TIP | Painted Niches

Choosing a color for the niche that is in contrast to the rest of the room will make the niche itself the focal point of the room. A color that is in the same color family as the rest of the room will highlight the object displayed within the niche.

niche was also a common element in the stucco- and adobe-walled homes of the Mission and Spanish Colonial styles. Today, prefabricated niches are available in a fairly broad range of styles. Adding a little paint and, of course, the right display piece can make one an appropriate accent for most homes.

Color selection makes the niches shown at left important elements in this home. The color connection is obvious, but also notice the gold leaf border that matches the detailing of the crown molding.

A fine example of niches flanking a passageway is shown opposite. These break up the large expanse of flat wall, and their shape echoes the arched doorway beyond.

WHERE TO PLACE A NICHE

As with a picture, a niche looks best when located on a proportionately sized wall. That is, small niches (which most are) can easily get lost or seem oddly insignificant against a large, flat wall area. There are exceptions to this rule, however, such as areas where the eye is naturally drawn, like the wall space opposite the top of a staircase or to the side of a passageway.

Best Locations. Because most niches project only a short distance from the wall, they work well as accent pieces in hallways and other confined areas. A stairway landing is another great location, where niches can house fixtures for decorative night-lighting or display a special piece that you enjoy seeing every day. A small space can be made more intimate by a single niche, while pairs of niches decorate on a larger scale. Placing one niche to either side of a passageway creates a pleasing three-part composition and a grand entrance. To the same effect, niche pairs can accentuate a significant piece of furniture or help define a more intimate space within a larger room area.

BUYING & INSTALLING A NICHE

Niches were traditionally made with stone, wood, or plaster, but today most readily available types are polyurethane foam or gypsum (drywall material). Designed for easy, do-it-yourself installation, most come prefinished (usually in white) and can be painted. One-piece models are the easiest to install and require no additional trim. You can also buy niche parts a la carte—typically the shell (recessed portion) and a one-piece trim surround with integrated shelf—allowing you to mix and match styles.

Some suppliers offer the top, half-dome portion of the shell intended for capping off a custom-built niche made with drywall or bent plywood. Standard-depth niches fit into regular 2×4 walls, but some types have a deeper recess. There are also surface-mounted niches that require no hole for installation.

Installation. The standard installation for one-piece niches involves cutting a hole in the wall's drywall and attaching the niche with glue and a few screws. Install smaller niches between wall studs without framing work. For larger models, or if the desired location coincides with

Stairways are great locations for niches, opposite. This is especially true of long winding stairs that have large expanses of wall space, such as this example. This niche presents a nice balance to the display of photographs.

This niche has to be large to compete with the grand architecture of the room, left, but its spare detailing is appropriate and welcome. A small statue of an angel adds a touch of humbleness.

a stud, you have to cut out the interfering portion of the stud(s) and add a header and sill to secure the niche. (That's for a non-load-bearing partition wall; alterations to a load-bearing wall require critical structural framing.) For a more custom project, you could buy a fabricated niche shell and build your own shelf, finishing the curved edge of the niche with flexible drywall corner bead, flexible mold-ing or an applied wood facing with a arched cutout.

Niches and niche parts are available through architectural products dealers and some millwork companies. Home centers and lumberyards don't typically carry niches in stock but will give you their suppliers' literature, and you can order through their store. You can also find suppliers on the Internet.

Niche or Nook?

These two terms are often used interchangeably. For the purposes of this book, a niche has gently sloping sides while a nook has sides that are more squared off. Despite having the arched top typical of a niche, the example shown here has the square sides of a nook, giving it a more casual look. Another difference: niches have a single shelf for display; nooks can have multiple shelves. This nook contains adjustable shelves.

Decorative Nooks

Decorative nooks are found in all types of houses—anywhere the architect or homeowner sees the need for an original detail or a special place for a favorite collection. As custom, built-in features, nooks can be designed to suit many applications and purposes. Their forms can range from simple, drywalled recesses with no trim to handcrafted, wood-lined cabinets with glazed doors. A nook may hold a single display item, as niches often do, or include an entire collection housed in a set of shelves and illuminated by recessed lights. Nooks can be practical, too: many early twentieth-century homes included nooks as telephone stands or small china cabinets.

Nook Locations. Like niches, nooks work well in hallways and other traffic areas, where they can have significant visual impact without encroaching on the space. But with their great flexibility of size, style, and configuration, nooks can be added to almost any type of room. An elaborate living room treatment might combine a variety of nooks on the same wall. A nook built above a fireplace mantel—a popular Craftsman detail—creates an interest-

ing yet unassuming overmantel and an ideal display space. Bathroom nooks are space-saving decorative features; with a mirrored interior and glass shelves, a nook provides a sparkling display for perfume bottles. In a kitchen, a shelved nook can fill the back side of an island beneath an overhanging countertop; and in a bedroom, a large nook rising from the floor suggests a cozy canopy arching over the head of a bed.

CONSTRUCTING A NOOK

There are no specific construction techniques or design guidelines for building a nook, since most are designed to fit a particular space. The simplest style is a square or rectangular wall recess composed of a 2×4 frame covered with drywall or one-by lumber. This basic design can be embellished with an arch top, molding along the edges, or a decorative shelf that

A deep nook with integrated lighting, opposite bottom, can be a significant architectural feature.

This clever recessed display nook, opposite top, is installed between two wall studs.

Nestled in a corner, above, a book-filled recessed cabinet sets the tone for a quiet reading space.

These custom cabinets, right, feature a built-in decorative nook above each unit. At 42 in. tall, the cabinets extend all the way to the ceiling and suffer no loss of storage space.

projects slightly from the wall. You can build a simple nook with a 4-inch recess by following the basic framing procedure shown in "Creating a Pass-Through," on page 79. The key difference is that for a nook, you cut out the drywall on only one side of the wall, using the back of the remaining drywall to serve as the back panel of the nook.

Deep Nooks. To create a deeper nook, build a box with ¾-inch plywood and secure it between two wall studs or within a frame like that of the pass-through. For finished inside surfaces, use paint-grade plywood and caulk the joints between pieces, or line the inside of the box with ¼-inch-thick drywall. Tape and finish the drywall seams, or cut carefully and apply a thin bead of caulk.

Finish the outside edges of a nook with wood molding or, for a cleaner look, drywall corner bead. Corner bead comes in standard square-edged type and rounded type (called bullnose), as well as in flexible versions used for arches.

A PEACEFUL, UNCLUTTERED PLACE

The concept of the nook in its purest, most decorative form is exemplified by the traditional Japanese design feature called a *tokonoma*. Found in most homes and traditional lodgings, the tokonoma is a large, recessed alcove often measuring 12 to 18 inches in depth and ranging in width from a few to over a dozen feet. Its design and decoration are minimal, with a low platform or floor made of fine wood, plain wall surfaces, and soft downlighting that highlights a hanging scroll on the back wall. The only other decoration is a simple vase (often holding a seasonal floral arrangement) and perhaps a small sculpture placed on the platform. The calming effect of the tokonoma is surprisingly profound, as the eyes are quickly drawn by the simple beauty of its inviolate, glowing interior. Using the same elements of soft lighting and simple decoration, you can create a similar effect with a smaller recessed wall nook.

A simple decorative nook, above, tastefully mimics the surrounding wall treatment, giving dominance to the fine silver collection.

Recessed downlighting, right, creates dramatic shadow lines within the nook.

Rather than using ordinary cabinets, opposite top, this expansive kitchen employs a series of recessed nooks for storing items.

A flush wall, opposite bottom, over a gas fireplace leaves ample room for a decorative nook. This one serves as both mantelshelf and overmantel.

Wall-Hung Decorative Shelves

A home's decor and furnishings may reveal a lot about the owner's taste, but it's the decorative items that tell the personal stories. People display their favorite pieces on shelves not only because they like to view them, but also because they want their homes to reflect their lives and experiences, and they want to share their prized mementos with guests. Decorative shelves hold conversation pieces and can themselves be worthy of comment and admiration. An attractive, well-built, and well-placed shelf is an instant focal point that adds architectural detail and, of course, a personal touch.

This crown molding shelf, above, includes a flat shelf top to increase its carrying capacity.

Worn layers of paint add even more character to an eye-catching piece, left. Graduated shelves subtly categorize their contents, adding to the visual appeal of the entire unit

Thick glass shelves fit perfectly over their decorative supporting brackets, opposite. The large brackets are made unobtrusive by their finish, which matches the wall's.

Shelf Locations. Decorative shelves are great decorating tools because they go almost anywhere. In addition to the obvious places, you can set them above doors and windows, in corners, over cabinets, above passageways, and along stairwells, or hang them from the ceiling. As long as it supports its contents, a shelf can be made with any material; it can be sized to hold a single bud vase or to wrap around an entire room.

SHELF MATERIALS

For a primer on shelving styles see "Types of Shelving," on page 118. In addition to the standard wood options (solid wood, plywood, particleboard, and MDF), decorative shelves can be made of glass, stone, marble, or metal. Glass is popular for its clean look and ability to transmit light.

Glass fabricators are the only sources of glass thick enough to be used for shelves (¼ inch is usually a minimum); they'll also recommend a thickness for your application, custom-cut the shelves to size, and finish the edges with a plain or decorative edge.

Other Materials. Stone, marble, and metal are less commonly used materials but can have a striking appearance. Flagstone has a warm, organic feel and is readily available through suppliers of landscaping materials. Granite and marble are cool and elegant. They're trendy materials for countertops but also make great shelves. Metal shelves can offer variously modern and industrial looks. Diamond plate, sheet aluminum, and iron are fairly easy to come by; getting a finished edge will require the help of a machine shop or metal fabricator.

Types of Shelving

Decorative shelves come in so many varieties that they are best categorized by their basic construction:

Bracketed Shelf. Bracketed shelves are the most common type—a flat shelf surface supported by right-angle brackets. Brackets of all descriptions can be bought at home centers and hardware and woodworking stores, and ornately decorated versions are available through millwork companies. Bracketed shelves are often built as one piece, with or without a back panel between or behind the brackets. When one-piece units have no back panel, a mounting cleat installed along the back shelf edge makes for easy installation.

Plate-Rail Shelf. A plate rail is typically considered a trim detail, but is in essence a decorative shelf. (See page 120.) With a narrow shelf usually supported by brackets or crown or cove molding, plate rail is used for displaying plates, framed pictures, etc. It has a groove cut into its top surface for holding the edges of plates.

Cleated Shelves. Cleated shelves are supported on the sides and back by one-by cleats secured to the wall. These are often used for storage shelves in closets but work well for decorative shelves if the cleats aren't too noticeable. They are a good option for rounded corner shelves.

Suspended Shelves. Suspended shelves hang from cables, chains, or all-thread (threaded rods) and have a distinctly contemporary look. They can hang freely from the ceiling or be supported by angled lengths of cable or chain secured to the wall.

Cantilevered Shelves. Cantilevered shelves have no visible supports, thus appearing to defy gravity. In reality, the shelf surface may be secured to the wall framing or installed as shown at far right. Installing cantilevered shelves is more complicated than installing other types, but the result is an exceptionally streamlined appearance with an artistic built-in quality.

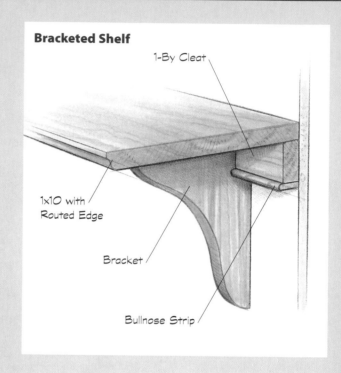

Bracketed Shelf

1-By Cleat

1x10 with Routed Edge

Bracket

Bullnose Strip

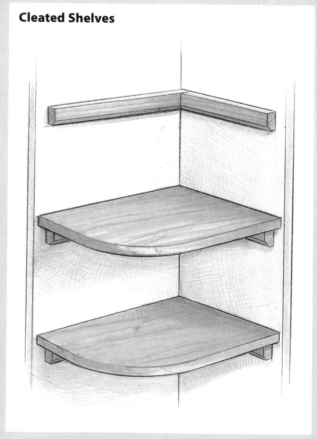

Cleated Shelves

Plate-Rail Shelf with Bracket

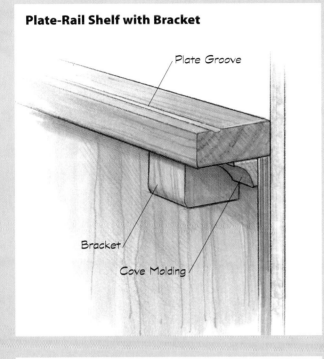

Plate Groove

Bracket

Cove Molding

Plate-Rail Shelf with Cove

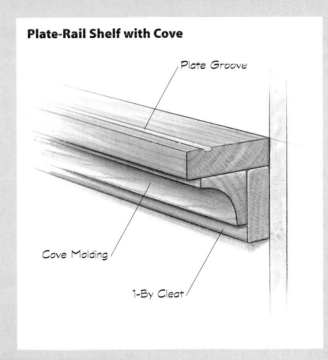

Plate Groove

Cove Molding

1-By Cleat

Suspended Shelves

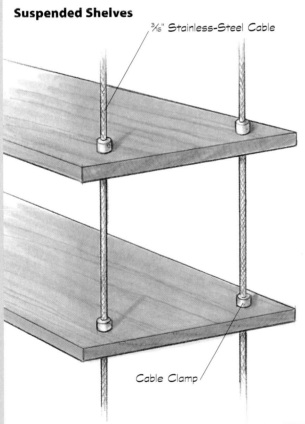

³⁄₁₆" Stainless-Steel Cable

Cable Clamp

Cantilevered Shelves

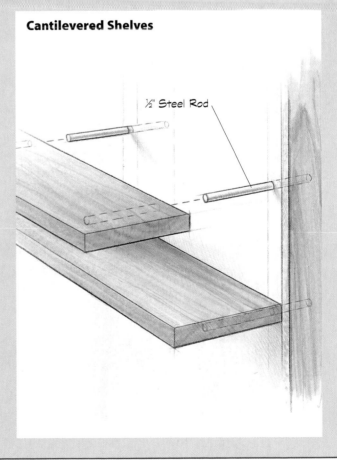

½" Steel Rod

Salvaged Shelves

One creative approach for adding new shelves is to use old parts. Architectural salvage yards are full of appealing items that make great decorative shelves—though not every one may look like a shelf at first glance.

Brackets and corbels are among the best options because their original purpose is to support a structure. Often carved with rich detail, brackets and corbels (found in wood, stone, and iron) work well as stand-alone shelves or as supporting brackets for a shelf top. A decorative header from an old door or window surround can become a beautiful one-piece shelf. With a little modification, you can make display shelves from some unlikely elements: a copper gutter can become a plate rail, and a section of exterior cornice can get a new life as an art display.

Without the side casings, above, this salvaged window header makes a unique decorative shelf.

Three salvaged ornaments, opposite, display plates in an interesting overmantel treatment.

Crown Molding Shelves

With its projecting angle and decorative profile, standard crown molding is a great shelf material. You can make a shelf like the one shown here with materials you purchase at the home center. Use two-by blocking and crown molding to create a plate shelf above your kitchen cabinets or above built-in cabinets in another room, or you can create a simple wall-hung shelf.

To make the shelf, bevel the front edge of a length of blocking that spans the width of the shelf and fasten it to the wall with screws. Countersink the screws. Install crown molding against the blocking, leaving a slight overhang at the top to serve as a plate groove, as shown at right. Be sure that the molding does not interfere with the operation of the cabinet doors. For a wall-hung shelf, add mitered returns to the ends of the crown molding.

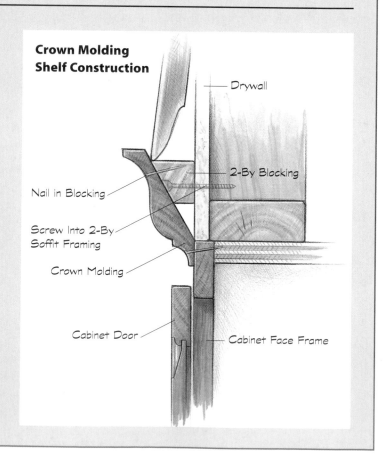

Crown Molding Shelf Construction

- Drywall
- 2-By Blocking
- Nail in Blocking
- Screw Into 2-By Soffit Framing
- Crown Molding
- Cabinet Door
- Cabinet Face Frame

Built-In Decorative Shelving

Built-in decorative shelves can be nothing more than a simple wood framework built onto a wall. In fact, it's often the case that simpler is better, because these types of shelves are meant for displaying their contents rather than being ornaments themselves. Like built-in bookcases, decorative shelves look great when recessed, but this is less of a concern because their shelves can be much shallower than bookshelves; strength is typically less important, too.

All of these characteristics make built-in decorative shelving a useful design element that is easy and inexpensive to build. You can use shelves to enhance oddly shaped walls, creating irregular spaces that conform to a sloping ceiling or a room transition. A row of see-

Built-in units bring efficiency to a small kitchen, right. The desk alcove relies on a pigeon-hole case for storage. Corner shelves complete a run of kitchen cabinets.

Nothing brings out the colors of display pieces better than plain white shelves, below.

Bringing a cathedral ceiling down to a cozier level, opposite, this false ceiling becomes an oversize decorative shelf above while creating a recess for a bank of built-in shelves below.

through cubbies spanning the top of a passageway can define the opening while bridging the spaces on either side. The same effect can be achieved with a single plank installed over a narrow wall opening. Anywhere a home's structure creates a nook or recess is an opportunity to add shelving: beside a projecting fireplace, above low foundation walls, along projecting beams and columns, or under and above wall cabinets.

Built-in shelves can be constructed piece-by-piece in the project area or using modular units built in a workshop and then installed and trimmed on-site. (See "Constructing a Basic Modular Bookcase," on page 136.) Cleated shelves offer easy installation for piece-by-piece projects, but for a clean look, it's best to support the shelves with screws driven through the upright pieces, or set the shelf ends in dados (grooves) cut into the uprights.

BUILT-IN BOOKCASES

uilt-in features add more to your home than economical storage space. While freestanding cases are merely furniture, built-ins are an integral part of the interior architecture, unifying the home's internal structure with the practical and aesthetic needs of everyday life. These are timeless details that have graced homes for centuries but have disappeared from most modern blueprints. Adding one to a home brings back a sense of craftsmanship and lends character to a generic floor plan. Most homes have at least a few good spaces for a built-in. Because a built-in unit can incorporate the floor, ceiling, and walls as parts of its structure, the construction is much simpler than that of stand-alone furniture—and usually much less expensive.

The Beauty of Built-Ins

Bookcases and shelving units may be simple, but they are far and away the most popular types of built-in. One reason for this must be that they house and display everyday things that people use but also like to look at: books, the good china, family photographs, artwork, curios—things that make a house a home. Another reason is that they can go virtually anywhere. Living and dining rooms, dens, and home offices are obviously good places for shelving, but so are entryways, kitchens, stairways, halls, and any tucked-away space created by intersecting walls or overhangs.

Fireplace walls are historically good locations for recessed shelving, because the projection of the fireplace creates either an alcove at either side or walls with nothing behind them. Similarly, attic spaces or second-floor bedrooms tucked under a roof often have short kneewalls that are perfect for recessed built-ins.

LIBRARIES

The love of books has led homeowners through the ages to build household shrines for keeping them and enjoying the quiet act of reading. Up to the mid-1800s, personal libraries were the propriety of the rich and were ornate showpieces for architects and symbols of a homeowner's learnedness. But by the late Victorian era, libraries were common features of middle-class homes, largely due to a rise in book production in America. Today the home library is a rarity. Even the sequestered den—a space that is half library, half office—has given way to the high-tech demands of the modern home office.

Reading Areas. A classic library is a luxury few homes have the space to afford, but a dedicated reading area can be much simpler. With the addition of a few built-in bookcases, any semiprivate corner can become a civilized and welcoming place. Likewise, a home office that looks like a

interesting views. Back-to-back units can serve each space differently. Low cases provide a partial barrier and a large display shelf on top. When not used as a room divider, a built-in wall can cover an entire side of a room, giving the unit a truly integrated look and creating a strong focal point for the room.

Narrow bookcase modules, opposite, are the basis for this interesting built-in. A crosspiece with pediment detail creates a niche at the center. Museum lights and a unique trim embellishment draw attention to the top.

Individual wall units, left, are tied together by continuous crown and baseboard moldings.

Because the roof angle creates a large cavity, below, attic or upper-floor kneewalls have ample space behind them for a recessed unit.

melamine-covered "storage solution" can gain a great deal of warmth from custom bookcases. Even traditional library systems are simpler than you might think. Most can be built with a series of modular bookcase units fastened together and trimmed with any combination of ornate details and molding.

THE BUILT-IN WALL

A plain wall is just a barrier, but a wall made up of shelves full of books and decorative pieces is a feast for the eyes, surrounding you with the comfort of a personal collection. Depending on their size and configuration, built-in bookcases can be used to provide any degree of separation between spaces, as well as a great deal of storage space.

Built-in walls can assume a variety of forms. Open shelves leave some visibility between spaces and create

KITCHEN BUILT-INS

Every kitchen has built-in cabinets, but what about a butler's pantry? Originally an entire room located just off the kitchen, a butler's pantry was scaled down over the years into a cabinet-and-cupboard unit commonly found in modest Victorian homes and Craftsman bungalows. The basic design resembles a dresser, with deep cabinets and drawers in the lower section, a counter surface, and shallow cabinets or shelves above. Behind the counter a backsplash about 16 inches tall, often made of beadboard, unites the lower and upper sections. Its use today is the same as it was in the 1800s—the cabinets and drawers store pottery, glassware, china, silver, pots and pans, and dry goods, and the counter holds serving dishes ready for the table. This is a great feature for a wall that links the kitchen with an eating area.

Kitchen Offices. Another useful feature for busy kitchens is a small office space, consisting of a built-in desk and chair with open shelving above. Tucked into an alcove or corner and separated from the main work areas, a kitchen office is a convenient place for placing a telephone and directories, writing down messages and grocery lists, and storing cookbooks, mail, and recipes.

CHINA CUPBOARDS

As early American colonists began to settle into more established residences, one of the first built-ins they included was a cupboard, or hutch, for storing and displaying china, pewter, and silver pieces. Although English in origin, the china cupboard has become a quintessentially Colonial emblem. Simple versions of the cupboard might follow a dresser design, with a cabinet box with doors in the lower portion, topped by a shelf or counter surface, and an upper portion of shallow, open shelves. Another popular style was the corner cupboard, with its triangular case made to fit into a corner. Elaborate examples of these included fine trimwork, scroll-cut shelves, and a domed-shell top. Cupboards in colonial homes were typically found in the main room—the center of domestic life—or built into the fireplace wall.

DECOR TIP **Kitchen Displays**

Most cabinet manufacturers offer cabinets with open shelves. Placed at the end of a peninsula or on an island, open shelving can hold cookbooks or be converted to display areas for collectibles.

An office workspace, above, can quickly become an essential part of a well-equipped kitchen. This trim unit combines a bookshelf, cabinets, and desk within a small corner area.

Corner china cupboards are typical Colonial-style details, opposite. This replica piece includes ornate neoclassical styling.

Shelving Basics

When planning a built-in bookcase or any type of shelving unit, the primary decisions you need to make involve the shelves—namely, what material to use, whether you want them fixed or adjustable, and if adjustable, how they will be supported. Because the shelves do most of the work, they'll have a great impact on how well your built-in suits your needs.

SHELF MATERIALS

Materials for basic wood shelves fall into three categories: solid wood, plywood, and particleboard or MDF. Solid wood shelves are attractive but relatively expensive in hardwood species. Their main advantages are that they do not require an edge band or nosing to hide the front edge, and the edge can be shaped or milled with a router for a decorative profile. Solid wood is also strong: a ¾-inch-thick shelf of average width can span about 34 inches

Built-in units, above, that serve doubly as bookcase and entertainment center offer practical placement of TV and stereo equipment while diminishing their presence within the room.

Short bookcases and a beamed ceiling, right, give this comfortable room a low center of gravity, encouraging quiet moments for reading.

ENTERTAINMENT CENTERS

Many people feel that the mere presence of a television makes a room casual. If there's not enough space for both a TV/family room and a formal living room, an entertainment center that completely hides the electronic equipment can help one room serve as both. An ideal design for a multipurpose room includes numerous shelves for books and collectibles and has large, integrated cubbies with doors for housing the TV and stereo components. Electronic equipment does require some special considerations, such as wiring, ventilation, effective sound transmission, and space flexibility for changing components.

and are suitable for painting only. The shelf edges can be shaped and do not need banding. However, a solid-wood nosing or apron increases their strength; without one, shelves can span only about 20 inches without support. Home centers and lumberyards carry precut shelves in 8 and 12 inch widths, usually with a rounded front edge. Some versions are coated with melamine, a plastic surface similar to a laminate countertop, but not as tough.

For long-spanning shelves, standard materials can be laminated into double layers, or you can construct torsion box shelves, made with a ladder-like framework of solid lumber or plywood strips sandwiched between plywood skins. This construction produces very strong shelves that can also be quite thick—appropriate for a contemporary look.

Framing a set of French doors, left, this pine built-in is perfectly integrated with its surroundings. A thoughtful collection of display pieces brings out the detail of the shelves.

A "built-in wall" creates two window alcoves, below, and plenty of decorative shelving. The same concept could be used to make a window seat surrounded by bookshelves.

without support. The disadvantages of solid wood are the price, as mentioned, and its relative instability. Solid material expands and contracts with humidity changes and can become warped, resulting in wobbly shelves. It has also become increasingly difficult to find wide boards that are flat when you buy them.

Plywood. Plywood is the all-around best shelf material. It's economical, dimensionally stable, and strong enough to span about 32 inches without support (¾ inch thickness). Plywood is available with paint-grade veneers as well as veneers of the popular hardwood species, such as oak, maple, walnut, and mahogany. The disadvantage of plywood is its layered edge. If rounded over with a router, the naked edge looks good on contemporary-styled units, but traditional shelves need an edge band of decorative nose molding, wood-veneer tape, or an apron of solid lumber. Hardwood plywood is the best material for exposed-edge shelves, because, unlike standard plywood, the internal plies have no voids.

MDF and Particleboard. Shelves made with particleboard and MDF are very common, particularly among factory-made units. These materials are easy to work with

Building Bookcases

Most built-in bookcases consist of a simple wood box, or carcase, that receives a wood face-frame to dress up the front edges. Large bookcases and library systems are typically made with multiple bookcases installed and trimmed to appear as a single unit. This modular-style construction makes building even elaborate systems a reasonable do-it-yourself project. The standard bookcase rests on the floor and attaches to the wall through the side and/or back panels. Units that hang above the floor can be built modular-style, as well, but with some modifications to beautify the underside of the case if it will be visible.

SHELF SUPPORTS

Adjustable or fixed is the eternal shelf question. The pros and cons for each are straightforward: adjustable shelves can be moved, of course, but their means of adjustment (standards, clips, pins) detract from the appearance of a bookcase, and building bookcases with adjustable shelves is more difficult than building those with fixed shelves. Fixed shelves stay where you put them but offer a somewhat more "built-in" appearance. And the truth is, adjustable shelves are quite convenient if you need them, but most people never move the shelves once they're set.

Adjustable Shelves. For built-ins, adjustable shelves can use a pin system or a standard system. Pin systems use the basic arrangement of holes and inserted pins that hold the shelves. Pins come in a variety of styles, including clip-in types that prevent tipping, rubber-padded brackets for glass shelves, and pins combined with metal sleeves that prevent the pin holes from wearing out. For do-it-yourself projects, drilling pin holes is made much easier by using a pegboard template as a drilling guide.

Standard shelf systems employ C-shaped metal tracks that are slotted to receive clips for supporting the shelves. Standards are strong but somewhat unattractive. They are much less conspicuous when color-matched to the bookcase and installed into dadoes (grooves) milled into the sides of the case.

LOCATING A BOOKCASE

Finding the right spot for a built-in bookcase involves a few factors. First, if it will be recessed, you'll have to choose a wall with space behind it, and preferably a non-load-bearing wall so you won't have to make major structural changes to create an opening for the recess. Often recess space can be borrowed from a little-used closet or a guestroom that can afford some encroachment of floor space.

Partially Recessed. Another option is to recess the case only partially, which will give the unit a built-in look and reduce its projection somewhat. To create a partial recess about 2 inches deep, remove the drywall on the unit-side of the wall and turn the wall studs flat against the back side of the opposing drywall. You can do this only on a non-load-bearing wall. If you're concerned about bookcases making a small room feel smaller, try to recess the cases even a little. Recessed cases tend to expand a space visually, while fully projected and freestanding units seem to close in on a room.

Unusual spaces are great for built-in bookcases because they make for clever use of an otherwise wasted or unadorned area. Oddly shaped spaces may require some custom construction, but it's often possible to start with a square or rectangular modular unit and add elements to fit the space.

By painting the shelf standards white and recessing them into the side pieces, opposite, the builder of this bookcase retained the traditional styling.

These recessed bookcases, left, look built in but are actually hanging (wall-mounted) shelves that take advantage of recesses in the fireplace wall. A continuous stock of books hides the supporting hardware.

With its modified classical details and brightly painted interior surfaces, below, this built-in provides a strong backdrop for an eclectic setting. Fixed shelves provide a built-in appearance.

CASE MATERIALS

For most bookcase projects, the material used for the carcase is the same as for the shelves. (See "Shelving Basics," page 130.) The most commonly used materials are ¾-inch-thick board lumber, plywood, or MDF, with ½-thick plywood used for the back panel. Bookcases with traditional styling also look good with a back panel made of tongue-and-groove beadboard (or you can use look-alike sheet versions). You may opt for a bookcase without a back panel. If so, the unit must be well attached to a supporting structure, as it will have very little lateral stability without a back panel.

SIZING THE SHELVES

The best way to determine the depth and spacing of your shelves is to measure the items that will go into the bookcase. Standard shelves are between 8 and 12 inches deep; 11 inches is deep enough to accommodate most books. Another consideration is economy: reducing the shelf size by a small amount can sometimes make the difference between having to buy one piece of plywood or two, for example. The shelf length determines the width of the bookcase but is itself subject to the strength limitations of the material. If the length exceeds the recommended span, you'll have to add intermediate supports between shelves.

Special Considerations. Thoughtful planning will help a built-in project go smoothly, but there are a few common pitfalls to keep in mind. Before making serious plans to add a recessed unit, make sure the wall receiving the bookcase contains no plumbing, wiring, or ductwork that would have to be moved. Unless you're removing a full-height section of the wall, you'll need to add a header and perhaps a sill to frame the opening and support the remaining drywall.

Few homes have a traditional library, but if you want one, the room shown opposite is a good model. The built-in bookcases that flank the mantle are more for display than book storage. Note how downlights illuminate the items on the top shelves.

This deep corner bookcase, right, is made less obtrusive by a set of end shelves.

DECOR TIP | **Bookcase Lighting**

Bookcases generally look and work best when brightened by some form of downlighting (that is, overhead lights pointed downward). Lights installed inside or just in front of the case are ideal because they illuminate the spines of the books and won't be blocked by someone looking closely over the titles. Today's low-voltage fixtures are a great option for bookcase lighting.

If you're building floor-to-ceiling modular cases, make them about 2 inches shorter than the ceiling so that you can tip the case into position. Hide the gaps below the ceiling with crown or other molding. Wiring for lights or speakers will be much harder to install after the cases go in, so plan ahead. Finally, never trust that walls, floors, and ceilings are straight, level, or plumb. Note where parts of the bookcase or trim will have to be scribed and cut to follow contours and uneven surfaces.

Constructing a Basic Modular Bookcase

The case shown here is made with ¾-inch plywood with a ½-inch-plywood back panel and a face-frame made of one-by hardwood boards. The shelves are attached with screws driven through the side pieces. Wood plugs hide the screw heads. If you want to install multiple units, add plugs to only the exposed sides of the end units.

Assembly. To build the bookcase, cut the side pieces ½ inch wider than the shelf depth, to create a recess for the back panel. Cut the shelves and top piece to size (shelves over 32 inches will require mid-supports). If desired, add nosing trim or veneer tape to hide the front edges of the shelves. Assemble the carcase with coarse-thread drywall screws driven through counterbored pilot holes. Cut the back panel; make sure the carcase is square; then attach the panel with glue and brads. Also nail through the back panel into the shelves. You can install 1 x 2 mounting cleats underneath the bottom shelf and above the top shelf for more strength.

Installation. Install the case by screwing through the mounting cleats and into the wall framing. Install the face-frame with glue and finishing nails. You can preassemble the frame using biscuits or install it one piece at a time. Add molding or one-by trim boards along the top and, if desired, along the bottom of the case. You can match the existing base molding to create a built-in look.

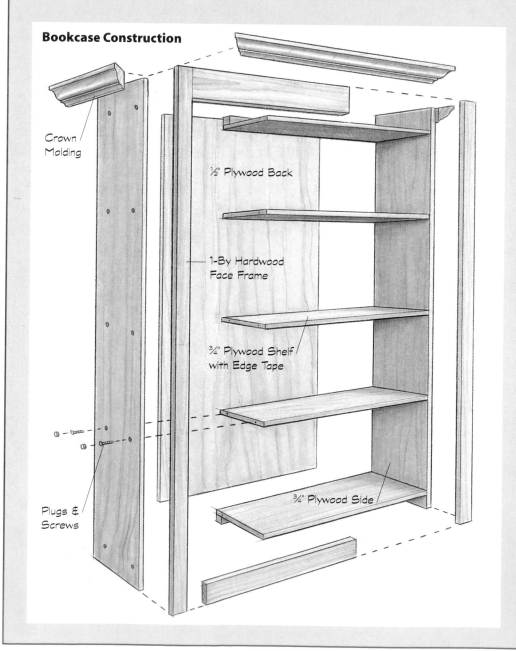

Bookcase Construction

Crown Molding

½" Plywood Back

1-By Hardwood Face Frame

¾" Plywood Shelf with Edge Tape

Plugs & Screws

¾" Plywood Side

Making Add-Ons Look Built-In

There are several tricks to fool the eye of even a careful observer. Trimwork is the best tool of deception because it hides gaps around modular shelving units and ties multiple units together into a seamless whole. It can also be used to decorate the built-in to match details elsewhere in the house. If a room has baseboard or crown molding, wrapping the same molding around the built-in will make it look like it was installed by the original builder. The illusion is most effective if the style of the built-in complements or blends with the character of the house. A rustic, knotty-pine cupboard won't look like an original part of a contemporary interior, just as a white melamine bookcase will stand out in any historical setting.

Recessing Strategies. Recessing a unit goes a long way to making it look built-in. Even a partial recess will help. If you can't cut into a wall to recess a unit, you can fur out the wall around the bookcase—that is, add a second wall layer of 2×4 studs (or even 2×2s) and drywall to build up the wall's thickness after the unit is installed. Another option that works for units that rise to within 18 inches of the ceiling is to build a soffit to fill the space between the unit and the ceiling, similar to the treatment applied above kitchen cabinets. The soffit can run straight up from the unit or be L-shaped, with the lower (horizontal) part of the L meeting the unit at a right angle. The latter design creates a box that can house recessed light fixtures that illuminate the front of the built-in.

Choosing a wood type or painted finish that matches other room elements is a good idea, but you can further enhance the built-in look with unit doors styled after interior room doors. Built-in doors that are glazed can be modeled after the home's windows. When units are completely recessed and trimmed, consider using the same casing that appears on windows and doors.

A discreet recessed bookcase, top right, gains architectural significance from an applied archway.

A small bookcase adds a cozy touch to this bedroom, right. The broad trim band unites the bookcase and suggests a ceiling line with a more human scale.

CHAPTER 9

CEILING TREATMENTS

A s the largest unused surface in any room, the ceiling is an ideal place for adding architectural detail. These are treatments that go far beyond the effects of standard texture, paint, and paper decoration. They add actual depth and dimension and, in some cases, illumination or a touch of architectural history. Ceiling features have undergone an interesting evolution over the years—from the rough timber beams of medieval and early Colonial homes to neoclassical Jeffersonian domes and the clean, geometric faces of a modern drywalled soffit. Many of these details are still available today in variously authentic and faux or decorative forms. Some are designed for quick installation; others are custom, built-in features.

Decorative Beams & Coffered Ceilings

Beamed and coffered ceilings have been in style since medieval times, when most of the beams were real and coffers were created by cross-beaming between the main structural members. After plaster ceilings became the norm, designers and builders turned to decorative beams and coffer treatments to dress up the plain, smooth surfaces. Each architectural period has produced its own variations of these bold, traditional features, and today's versions are built much like their predecessors.

DECORATING WITH BEAMS

Decorative beams add a heavy, structural look, but this is merely an illusion. While some applied beams are actual solid timbers (typically used for rustic interiors), most are constructed of simple, hollow boxes adorned and bolstered with trim moldings. The basic construction of beams is discussed on page 142.

Because beams form parallel lines spanning from side to side in a room, they tend to emphasize the room dimension to which they are parallel. That is, beams running lengthwise make a room appear longer, while those running sideways make a room seem wider. Cathedral ceilings make beams soar upward toward the high peak. Generally, beams work best in large rooms, where their heft and boldness can assume a grand scale. Bathrooms, hallways, and entryways, for example, can be crowded by a beam treatment. That said, beams also have a sheltering quality and can be used to create a cozy, intimate atmosphere in smaller or low-ceilinged spaces. Early Colonial homes certainly had low ceilings, and the structural beams overhead made their rooms comfortable instead of oppressive.

Locations for Beams. As custom-built features, beams can be almost any size or style, and so can be made to suit a variety of applications. Living rooms and family rooms are the most popular locations for beams, followed by dining rooms and kitchens. In bedrooms, beams can be used for their sheltering quality or simply to make a plain ceiling more inter-

esting to look at while you're lying in bed. Beams in kitchens often have a rough-hewn or structural look, perhaps referring to the long history of the kitchen as a work area, before it became the polished gallery of appliances it is today.

Simple box beams, opposite left, painted to match a room's trimwork can be a significant feature that complements the decor without dominating it.

Decorative beams and columns define a bar area, opposite right. Low-voltage lights set into the hollow beam boxes provide accent lighting.

A monochromatic paint job softens the visual impact of the beams, left, while a matching band along the wall adds importance to the ceiling treatment.

The look of traditional post-and-beam framing, below, can be replicated with decorative beams made from reclaimed solid timbers.

Decorative Beam Construction

Most decorative beams are not solid but rather hollow, C-shaped channels made with three finish boards and applied molding. It's this construction that gives them the common name "box beam." Box beams are made today pretty much as they have been for hundreds of years. A bottom face board is joined at its edges by two side boards to create the basic box. The joints may be grooved (with rabbets and dados), mitered, or simply butted.

Basic Construction. The box frames are typically built in a workshop, then installed and trimmed on the ceiling. Installing the boxes is easy: first, a two-by lumber cleat is fastened to the ceiling joists following the beam layout. The box frames are fitted over the cleats and secured with glue and finishing nails. Molding is then added as embellishment to the boxes and to hide any gaps. Where beams run parallel with ceiling joists, the beam layout must follow the joist spacing, or you can install blocking between the joists (most easily done from above the ceiling) to support the cleats. Beams running perpendicular to joists have no such layout limitations.

End Treatments. There are a number of possibilities for treating the ends of the beams. They can meet walls at a wide trim board installed along the room's perimeter, or their ends can rest on brackets or corbels mounted to walls. The typical treatment for walls parallel with the beams is to add half-beams that appear to be partially covered by the wall. The same effect can be created at perpendicular walls, with a relatively larger beam that appears to support the ends of the regular beams. A third option is to incorporate a partial-beam detail into a built-up cornice treatment. Rough beams that run straight into end walls replicate the traditional practice of concealing post-and-beam house framing behind fields of plaster.

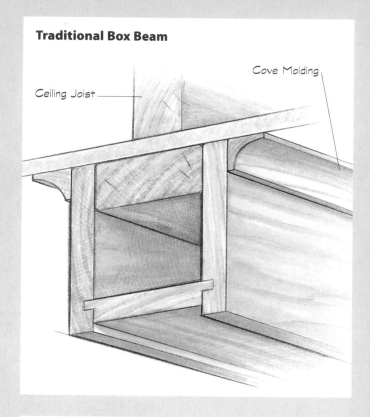

Traditional Box Beam

Ceiling Joist

Cove Molding

Butted Box Beam

Ceiling Joist

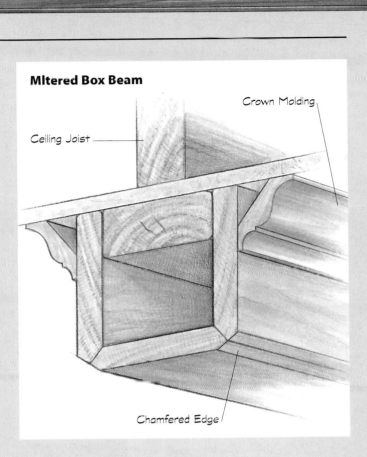

Mitered Box Beam

Crown Molding

Ceiling Joist

Chamfered Edge

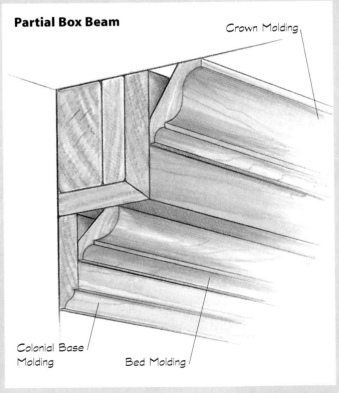

Partial Box Beam

Crown Molding

Colonial Base Molding

Bed Molding

Finishes for Beams. When it comes to finishes, richly stained wood embodies the most classic look for beams. Dark stain on beams against a light-colored ceiling brings great contrast, while lighter beams over a background of a similar wood paneling add a warm and organic feel. Painting beams can bring out contrasts or highlight details, or make beams blend with the surroundings. Rough-hewn beams look good when left bare or when given a diluted color wash that accentuates the coarse texture of the wood.

Not all beam treatments have to mimic structural framing. Used individually, beams can create borders that delineate space, suggest thresholds and decorate passageways, or house recessed lighting fixtures. Individual beams become more decorative and architecturally balanced when supported (visually at least) by brackets, columns, or pilasters.

One traditional design touch is to make it appear as if the beam is supported by brackets or corbels.

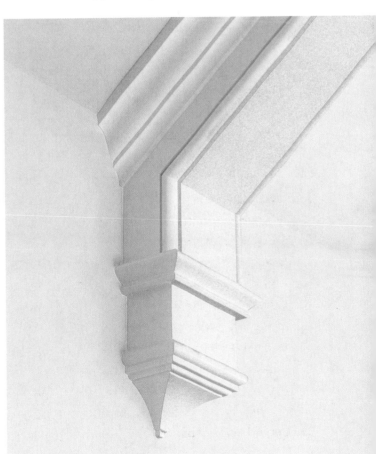

COFFERS

By definition, a coffered ceiling is any of a variety of treatments consisting of a projecting grid framework that creates a series of uniform recessed panels. The term "coffer" actually refers to the panel created by the framework. The Romans conceived the idea and built coffers into the Pantheon, and the treatment has since been adopted by many period styles in a variety of forms.

The original classical coffers were plaster and often had highly ornamented frames and panels. Today they can be made with such easy-to-install materials as drop-in ceiling

TRIM TIP | **Ceiling Heights**

Deep, traditional coffers look best on high ceilings for two reasons: first, coffers attached to a low ceiling will make the room feel cramped; second, when installed on a high ceiling—9 feet high or higher—most of the grid design is usually visible from any point in the room.

tiles, but the classic coffer treatment, which follows medieval designs, consists of decorative wood beams and crossbeams laid over a flat ceiling.

An Air of Formality. Coffered ceilings create a formal atmosphere, but they are not without warmth. In general, they tend to feel more decorative than beams and appear less structural than ornamental. There is something about recessed, geometric forms that appeals to the human eye, and the visual effect of an entire ceiling with such decoration is captivating. As with beams, the size and overall visual presence of a coffer grid should be in scale with the room it occupies.

Locations for Coffers. In historic interiors, coffered ceilings overlooked formal dining rooms, libraries, grand parlors, and living rooms. Coffers, as well as beams, were especially popular in Craftsman homes, owing to the period's affinity for medieval building forms. Craftsman designers often hung pendant light fixtures from the

A grid of wood trim on a diagonal layout, opposite, creates an eye-catching coffered effect.

Colonial styling, above, dictates a structural-looking coffer grid in this Revival interior. Note the color contrast between the beams and the plaster ceiling.

intersections of crossing beams. The compartmentalized layout of coffers also appealed to Victorian decorators, who added ornate molding to the members and dressed the panels with wallpaper.

Creating a coffered ceiling is the same as building and installing box beams, except with a grid layout. (See page 142.) Shop-built boxes are added in a parallel series across the entire ceiling; then cross beams are built to fit in between. The molding goes up after the beams are in place and helps to tie the grid together visually. Coffers typically include a half-beam treatment around the room's perimeter, creating a solid frame around the entire grid.

ing the roofing material (shingles), sheathing, and any insulation. The rafters are then covered on the top side with tongue-and-groove boards or other finish material that will make an attractive ceiling surface. Over the finish boards go a layer of rigid insulation and a deck of sheathing, followed by new shingles.

Uncovering a ceiling frame below an unused attic is a great way to open up a room and create a structural ceiling. Ceiling frames are typically built with 2×6 or larger joists. They are an important part of the roof structure and should not be removed without professional guidance. A remodel like this might include framing modifications to minimize the number of joists. With the ceiling surface removed, the view expands into the attic, where a skylight can be added for natural lighting and the underside of the roof frame can be finished to improve its appearance and reflect light.

Structural Ceilings

Structural ceilings take advantage of the inherent aesthetic quality of house framing. Roof structures, ceiling joists, and floor frames can be quite beautiful when uncovered. This practice has been used for centuries and actually predates the ceiling: in single-story medieval-style homes, rooms were open from the floor to the bottom of the roof. The ridge beam, rafters, and underside of the roof covering served as the ceiling. Modern building design requires insulated ceilings for energy efficiency, but these days the insulation can go on the outside of the roof structure (instead of between the rafters).

Exposing the Framing. Some home designs, such as post-and-beam, or timber-frame, styles are built with structural ceilings in mind. Creating the effect in ordinary stick-frame houses is usually an option only during a major remodel. Exposing roof framing yields the most dramatic results, because the angles of the roof naturally form a cathedral ceiling. A typical project involves remov-

Exposing Ceiling Joists. Exposing joists is relatively easy, but the frame often needs some work to become an attractive ceiling. One issue is the subfloor material above. Older homes have one-by board subflooring laid diagonally across the joists. This can look good with a little paint or stain, provided there aren't a lot of nails coming through. Newer homes have plywood subfloors, which can sometimes be painted but usually should be covered with a finish material. The spaces between floor joists often hold pipes, wiring, and ductwork, all of which can be moved, but at an expense.

A diluted white wash, opposite left, turned this exposed-joist frame into a rustic structural ceiling.

When adding on, it makes sense to utilize the space under the roof, opposite right. This addition features a structural ceiling design with attractive beam rafters.

Departing from the standard wood treatment, above, a series of decorative iron rods suggests the framing of the structure, and serves a structural purpose. Cables may be used instead.

Stripped down and cleaned up, left, a traditional roof frame reveals stunning beauty.

Soffits & Recesses

Soffits and recesses are built-in features that add depth and interest to a ceiling. Whereas beams, coffers, and applied accents decorate the surface, soffits and recesses alter the ceiling plane, making it a more dynamic architectural detail.

DESIGNING A SOFFIT

Most homes have some form of soffit, usually above the kitchen cabinets. A basic soffit is an L-shaped frame built into the corner where a wall meets a ceiling, and is typically covered with drywall. As functional elements, soffits can hide utility lines and structural beams, bridge the gap between a ceiling and a tall built-in or a bank of wall cabinets, or house recessed light fixtures. As design features, they can be used to customize a ceiling or simply to provide decorative detail.

By lowering the ceiling plane over specific areas of a room, a soffit can enhance the sense of shelter to make a space more cozy and intimate. Extending a soffit around the perimeter of the room creates a recess in the ceiling's center and an illusion of greater height. A soffit that meets columns or pilasters becomes an integrated beam element that can serve as a decorative feature or a room divider. And soffits don't have to be square-edged boxes. A shelf-style soffit projecting from a wall is a perfect place for concealed lighting that makes the entire ceiling glow.

SMART TIP Steel Soffits

For soffits, light-gauge steel framing is better than wood: it's lighter and straighter and requires fewer, shorter screws for installation. It's also fireproof—an important consideration when light fixtures are involved. Steel studs, tracks, and angles are available at home centers in standard 1⅝-, 2½-, and 3⅝-inch widths.

BUILDING A SOFFIT

A simple soffit consists of a ladder-like frame of 2x2 or 2x4 wood or light-gauge steel framing covered with ⅜- or ½-inch drywall. The frames can be prebuilt in a workshop or installed piece by piece in the project area. If the ceiling and walls are already finished, the soffit frame can go right over the existing surface and attach to the underlying framing. Soffits installed in corners need only two framed sides, while styles that drop from the ceiling or project from a wall require three sides. After the framing is in place, light fixtures can easily be added; then the frames are drywalled, taped, and finished to match the surrounding surfaces.

A grand treatment for an extraordinary space, left. This ceiling features a perimeter soffit with recessed lights; two octagonal trim lines restating the theme; and a simple, round medallion as a perfect centerpiece.

A shelf-style soffit, above, adds a human scale to this entryway and washes the upper ceiling area with a soft, inviting light.

Unique soffit features are great details for contemporary interiors, below.

Curved soffits can be framed with plywood or standard steel track cut and shaped to follow the contours, or with special flexible steel track designed for making curves (available at drywall supply outlets). Drywalling most curves is easiest with two layers of ¼-inch flexible drywall.

Soffits of all shapes must conform to local building codes regarding fire safety. As enclosed, hollow spaces, soffits typically must have fireblocking (either solid material or insulation) installed every 10 feet. Where soffit framing ties directly to ceiling or wall framing, with no drywall in between, fireblocking is used to seal the joist or stud spaces from the soffit cavity.

Building a Framed-In Recess

Building a framed-in recess is a fairly complicated project, but the result is a striking ceiling treatment rarely found in any but high-end custom homes. The project illustrated here works only on ceilings below an accessible attic space. To build the recess, add temporary supports under the joists at both sides of the planned opening. From the attic, install double joists to frame the sides of the recess (or add a sister joist to each existing joist that will serve as a side). Cut off the intermediate joists, and support them with headers at the ends of the recess. Add joists and nailers to create a ceiling for the recess. For a deeper recess, build up the depth of the original joists by adding a two-by frame, then install the recess joists and nailers. From below the ceiling, cut out the recess opening and wrap the insides of the frame with drywall. Add corner bead to the outside corners, and tape and finish the drywall.

Ceiling Recess Construction

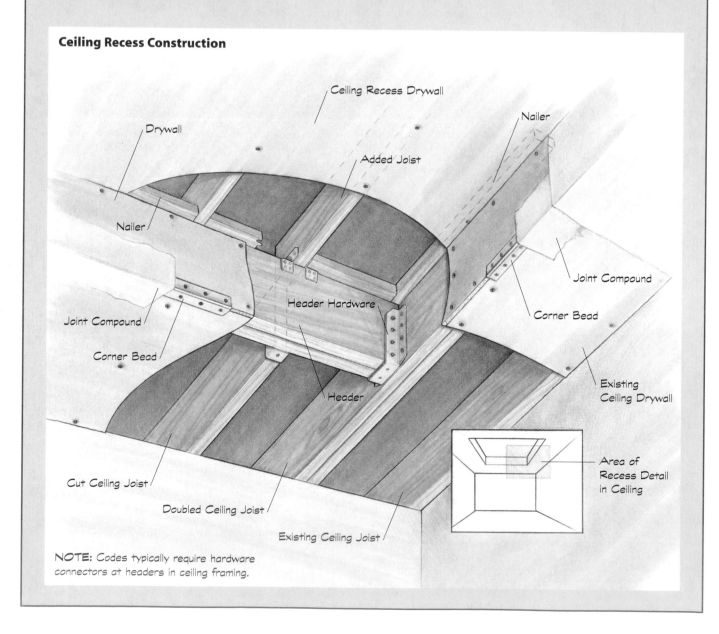

Ceiling Recess Drywall

Nailer

Drywall

Added Joist

Nailer

Joint Compound

Joint Compound

Corner Bead

Corner Bead

Header Hardware

Existing Ceiling Drywall

Header

Cut Ceiling Joist

Doubled Ceiling Joist

Existing Ceiling Joist

Area of Recess Detail in Ceiling

NOTE: Codes typically require hardware connectors at headers in ceiling framing.

DOMES

Ceiling domes are elegant, recessed ornaments traditionally found in finer rooms and grand entryways of historic neoclassical interiors. They can be used as focal points over a dining-room table or as centerpieces within great-room ceilings. As an anchor for a hanging light fixture, a dome becomes an eye-catching showpiece. Domes were traditionally made of plaster but today are available in one-piece polymer designs that install easily with adhesive.

Adding a dome is easiest in ceilings that have no floors above. To accommodate the recessed projection, an average-size dome requires an opening in the ceiling between 3 and 4 feet and a cavity between 7 and 12 inches deep. You can create the recess by cutting out a section of the ceiling joists and securing the loose ends with headers, similar to the construction shown in "Building a Framed-In Recess," opposite. With the framing complete, you cut out the drywall to the specified size and glue the dome in place.

Dome Styles. Domes are available through architectural products dealers and come in a variety of styles. Some have integral molding around the rim, and some are flush-mounted with no molding. The inside dome surface may be smooth or patterned, or it can be embellished with the addition of a ceiling medallion. Some manufacturers offer elliptical shapes in addition to standard round domes. Large prefab domes can be 7 feet in diameter and over 15 inches deep. Most types can be painted.

This clever ceiling detail combines a circular soffit with a prefabricated dome, above. The soffit projection creates the cavity for installing the dome.

When painted to match the ceiling, right, a flush-mounted dome recedes seamlessly from the surface.

MEDALLIONS

Medallions are classic ceiling accents and were used extensively by decorators from the early eighteenth century to the beginning of the twentieth century. With their rich detailing and ornate, deep-relief patterns, medallions were especially favored by the Victorians, who added them to the most principal rooms of the house. Traditionally, the size and level of detail of a medallion reflected the importance of the room as well as the status of the household. Medallions, like domes, are often featured above hanging light fixtures in a highly complementary arrangement. Also like domes, early plaster medallions are now being replicated in lightweight synthetic materials.

Installation. Architectural products dealers carry medallions in a wide range of sizes and styles. Installing one couldn't be simpler: mark the desired location on the ceiling; run a bead of adhesive over the medallion's back side; then tack it in place with a few nails. To add a light fixture, cut a center hole, using a handsaw or jigsaw, before installing the medallion. (Some models even come with a precut hole.)

Applied Ceiling Accents

Since the days when ceiling timbers were first covered with a layer of plaster, architects and designers have been devising ways to make plain ceilings more interesting. Many of the best—and easiest—techniques used today are traditional. In a modern home, where a ceiling often consists of a spray texture and a drab coat of paint, even the most basic accent can add a great deal of style.

TRIMWORK

Trimwork can do as much for ceilings as it does for walls—even more, because ceiling trim is so unexpected. Plain ceilings provide an empty canvas for decorative lines of molding, and here there really aren't any rules of form or application. A molding treatment can highlight a central feature, such as a medallion or chandelier, by radiating outward from the center in progressively larger bands. The finest historic interiors often used plaster ribbing to add ceiling detail, but a similar effect can be accomplished with moldings installed in the manner of wall frames. The frames can be painted to bring up the contrast and decorated inside with wallpaper or stenciling.

TIN CEILINGS

Traditional stamped-metal ceiling tiles have recently seen a rebirth as home decorations. The treatment originally flourished around the turn of the twentieth century, when it was used to cover high ceilings in Victorian-style homes (great for hiding cracked plaster), as well as for wainscoting on walls. Today's tiles look much as they did a hundred years ago, and there's a surprisingly large variety of styles

A grouping of applied ornaments creates a unique medallion, opposite.

This reproduction Victorian ceiling, below, was created from readily available tin tiles and trim pieces.

from which to choose. Readily available from specialty manufacturers, tiles come in 2×2- and 2×4-foot pieces, in materials including bare and prepainted steel; steel covered with tin, copper, chrome, and brass; plastic; fiberglass; and gypsum.

Tin tiles are a natural choice for kitchens, where the clean, metallic finish of the tile complements the many polished surfaces. They work well in bathrooms for the same reason, but there tiles must have a rustproof finish to protect against moisture damage. In large living areas, a full-ceiling tile treatment can be too busy for the relaxed atmosphere. As an alternative, you can accent specific areas with patches of tiles.

Installing a tile ceiling is straightforward but time-consuming. Traditional-style tiles are nailed to a layer of plywood or a grid of furring strips laid over the old ceiling. Cornices must be coped at inside corners and mitered at outside corners. Some tiles, commonly called "lay-in," are designed to fit into a standard suspended ceiling grid.

CHAPTER 10

COLUMNS & PILASTERS

*C*olumns and pilasters are among the few most important and enduring details of ancient architecture. They are fundamental construction forms, yet they represent a perfect combination of strength and beauty—they symbolize architecture itself. After two and a half millennia, columns and pilasters remain highly popular interior elements, appearing in everything from door surrounds to room dividers and serving as table bases, decorative shelves, and novelty pieces. They have been adapted in appearance to fit most interior settings: Georgian, Federal, and Greek Revival styles all made generous use of the refined classical models of Palladio and others, while Victorian and Craftsman designers created stylistic variations to suit their individual design schemes.

Columns

Technically speaking, a column is a vertical support member, usually installed under a horizontal beam, archway, or roof structure. As such, even purely decorative columns retain a structural look: when extending from floor to ceiling they appear to support the beam or ceiling structure above. Even freestanding columns convey a sense of strength and stability.

As a design element, a column defines a point in space. A single column is an architectural feature unto itself and can serve as an obstacle or part of an implied barrier, or can become a lone decorative item, like a sculpture to be viewed in-the-round. Two or more columns placed near each other suggest a spatial boundary, delineating interior areas or creating a threshold through which one can freely pass. An extension of this idea is the colonnade, a series of regularly spaced columns that creates a wall plane that is both permeable and architecturally dynamic. Whether by themselves or in groups, columns are especially effective details for open floor plans.

Column Types. Classical columns as a rule are round, but the basic form has assumed many shapes and styles over the years. For example, Craftsman builders, who used columns liberally throughout their interiors, built them with a characteristically square shape that tapered toward the top end. A dark wood stain contributed to a markedly un-classical appearance, yet the essential functions and appeal of the column form remained true. Today, most column manufacturers offer a standard range of classically inspired columns and perhaps a few alternative styles, such as octagonal or spiral shapes; finding something unusual might require a thorough search.

Post-and-beam construction relies on the column as both structure and ornament, opposite. This home shows the beauty of living among the framework.

Pedestals add structure, left, in this high-ceilinged home. Low wainscoting on the central, monolithic wall matches the pedestal detailing and contributes to a colonnade effect.

Columns should be sized appropriately for their application. Although purely decorative, the massive columns below look strong enough to carry the "weight" of the tall wall.

ANATOMY OF A CLASSICAL COLUMN

The column is found all over the world, but no one has done more with it than the ancient Greeks and, later, the Romans. So successful were the early designs that they are still followed in precise detail by column makers today. Of course, the rules have been bent somewhat, but the ancient classical style is by far the most popular and commonly available type of column. If you're planning to add traditional columns to your home, you'll probably be asked which style, or order, you prefer, so it helps to have some background.

The basic column form includes three main parts: the base, the shaft, and the capital. The appearance and style of each of these parts (particularly the capital) indicates the column's order. Three orders came from the Greeks: Doric, Ionic, and Corinthian; two came from the Romans: Tuscan and Composite.

Doric Columns. Doric columns are the oldest and simplest in form and are the only ones that have no base. Their shafts have shallow fluting, or grooves, that meet at sharp edges. Doric capitals are plain, with one rounded or ogee-shaped section topped by a square-edged plinth.

Ionic Columns. Ionic columns have a rounded base and a capital with distinctive scrolls, called volutes. Their shafts typically are fluted with deep, round-bottomed grooves, each separated by a flat edge along the perimeter of the shaft.

Corinthian Columns. Corinthian columns are the most ornamental of the Greek orders. They have a traditional rounded base and fluted shaft, like Ionic columns, but a highly ornate capital made up of rows of flaring acanthus leaves and pairs of volutes meeting at the top corners.

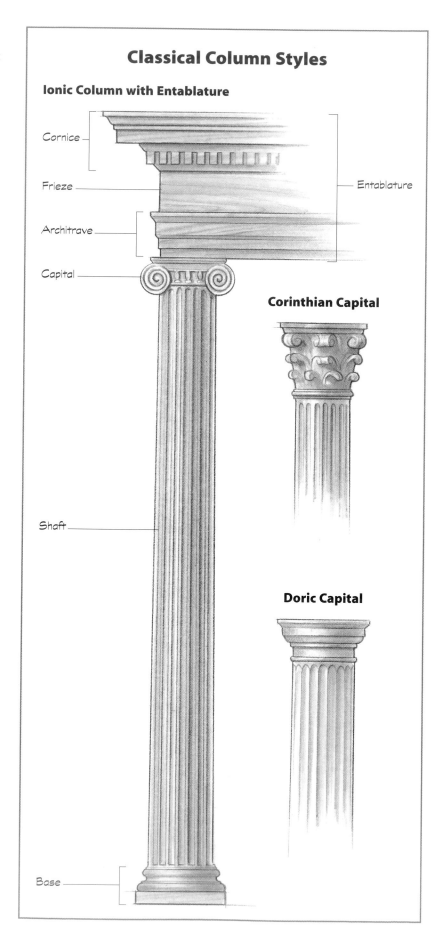

Classical Column Styles

Ionic Column with Entablature

Cornice

Frieze

Architrave

Capital

Entablature

Corinthian Capital

Doric Capital

Shaft

Base

Tuscan Columns. Tuscan columns are a variation of the Doric but with a rounded base and usually a band of half-round molding beneath the capital.

Composite Columns. Composite columns are a mix of styles. They combine elaborated forms of the Corinthian order with Ionic elements.

In classical architecture, columns typically supported a horizontal structure called an entablature, itself composed of three parts: the architrave, a band of moldings along the bottom; the frieze, a flat middle section; and the cornice, a projection of graduated moldings decorating the top of the entablature. The styling and construction details of entablatures correspond to the specific orders. Columns with entablatures have appeared in homes throughout history, including in modern interiors. The most common examples today are found in room dividers, fireplace mantels, and window and door surrounds. Another ancient feature that exists today is the pedestal, a decorated foundation beneath a column. These are frequently used as part of a room divider. (See page 166.)

The early designers of columns established rigid building specifications; namely, the relative sizes of the main parts and the style of fluting and other ornamentation. For those who want authenticity, some column manufacturers offer pieces that adhere to the old rules. Because the overall height of the column dictates the various dimensions, authentic replica columns must be custom-built for your application. Authentic columns should also be designed with a gradual tapering from bottom to top. This ingenious device, called entasis, solves a problem peculiar to columns—that a shaft with a uniform diameter will appear to the eye to be more slender at its middle than on its ends. Greek columns taper from the base to the capital, while Roman versions are straight along the bottom third of the shaft and tapered along the top two-thirds. Entasis may be nearly imperceptible in some cases, yet it gives columns a sculptural quality and an appearance of greater strength.

Columns with entablatures, left, add a classical touch to modern interiors. Note how the width of the column tapers toward the top.

Natural-grain wood columns are a common feature of Craftsman-inspired schemes. The square shape and simple base and capital moldings, below, are typical of the style.

COLUMN MATERIALS

The Greeks built columns from marble and other types of stone; to this materials list modern builders have added wood, plaster, fiberglass, polyurethane, polystyrene foam, metal, and cast stone. Most columns are made in three pieces—base, shaft, and capital—and often with different materials used for each piece. This not only makes the column less expensive, it allows you to mix and match parts of your own choosing.

Wood is the most common material for shafts and may be paint-grade or stain-grade. Paint-grade shafts are made with staves—small pieces of wood interlocked with finger joints to create a strong, hollow cylinder. Stain-grade shafts are made with full-length strips of wood joined so

DECOR TIP   Creative Columns

A single freestanding column that stops short of the ceiling makes an impressive accent piece. Use a mid-size column as a plant stand, phone table, pedestal for a light fixture, or display stand for a bust or other artwork. Short, stout columns with broad tops work well as table bases or legs, nightstands, or end tables.

that their coloring and grain patterns match, creating the appearance of a solid piece. Small or slender columns may be cut from a single piece of solid wood. Square columns can be built with board lumber, plywood, or MDF.

Bases and Capitals. Bases and capitals are made from a variety of materials, including polyurethane, fiberglass, and a composite of fiberglass and plaster. Because capitals can be highly ornate, modern materials and molding techniques are used to make the look of hand-carved detailing affordable. Some manufacturers offer bases and plain capitals in wood and cast marble, but at a premium cost.

While most interior columns are purely decorative, some can be used in load-bearing applications. An example of this is a project in which you remove a load-bearing wall and replace it with a structural beam supported by a number of columns. For this type of application, you can use columns that are engineered for the project or install adjustable steel columns (like the ones found in basements) and hide them with split decorative columns that you glue together around the steel member. The latter are a great option for basement-finishing projects.

Clearly this archway, left, was designed with this column treatment in mind. The stylized classical detailing of the columns is in keeping with the artistic urn fixtures and garland-covered cornice.

A contemporary colonnade, opposite, borrows from classical design. The last column in this series is actually a pilaster built into the wall corner.

INSTALLING A COLUMN

Installing a decorative column is usually a simple and straightforward project. The proper method varies based on the column material and application, so it's best to follow the manufacturer's installation instructions. A typical installation starts with using a plumb bob hung from the beam or ceiling to mark a point directly below it on the floor. The base is then secured to the floor, centered on the mark. Next, the shaft is installed on top of the base and may or may not have the capital attached. Finally, the capital is secured to the ceiling or beam above (and to the shaft, if not already secured).

In some cases, the base and capital are attached to the floor and ceiling, respectively, then the shaft is cut to fit in between. Other installations involve base and capital rings that slip over the ends of the shaft. After the shaft is secured to the floor, the rings are slid into place and fastened to the shaft.

Pilasters

The pilaster may be less well-known by name than the column, but it has an equally important place in interior architecture. In fact for the average home, pilasters have many more uses than columns. By definition, a pilaster is a flat, square-edged pier or column that is attached to a wall. Because it projects from the wall a distance equal to a third of its width (or less), a pilaster has the appearance of a full, square column that was embedded into the wall, with only its front portion left exposed. Some of the earliest pilasters actually were embedded columns (or masonry projections that helped support an arch), but now this structural aspect is merely an effective illusion. Like a column, a pilaster has a base, shaft, and capital.

ANATOMY OF A PILASTER

Pilasters were favorite elements of the ancient Romans and Italian Renaissance builders. Like columns, they follow the classical orders in design, but accurate replication today is less common than with column construction. Essentially a pilaster is a composition of trim elements attached to a wall or other flat surface. For added projection, some parts are built up behind with shims or blocking to increase the depth.

Plinth Blocks. Pilaster bases typically include a flat block called a plinth. The plinth should be deeper and wider than the pilaster's shaft. Above the plinth a band of molding wraps around the bottom end of the shaft, mimicking the appearance of a simple column base. When a

pilaster shaft starts well above the floor, the base often resembles a square column pedestal that may have a decorated or paneled face.

The most common type of pilaster shaft is a straight board with flutes cut into the face, although many are blank or contain a recessed panel. Flutes in the classical vein are closely spaced and all have the same length; an alternative style, sometimes called Victorian fluting, has fewer (usually three) wide flutes, with the central groove extending beyond the ends of the outer grooves. Some shafts are tapered from bottom to top, which can lend an appearance of strength. Below the bottom of the capital, shafts frequently bear a collar or narrow band of molding. Capitals are often made with crown molding and other trim and have an angled profile similar to a ceiling cornice. Classically styled versions might have ornate capitals with Ionic or Corinthian detailing.

DECOR TIP | Faux Finishes

Try marbleizing wood columns to make them look like the real thing. Other faux-finish effects include aging, patinating, or adding painted-on flutes or horizontal lines to imitate segmented construction.

Pilaster Applications. As close cousins of the column, pilasters frequently appear with entablatures, most commonly in such locations as fireplace mantels and door and window surrounds. In other applications, pilasters form the vertical supports in archways or tie into a ceiling cornice. Pilasters are usually made of wood or a synthetic material such as polyurethane or polystyrene.

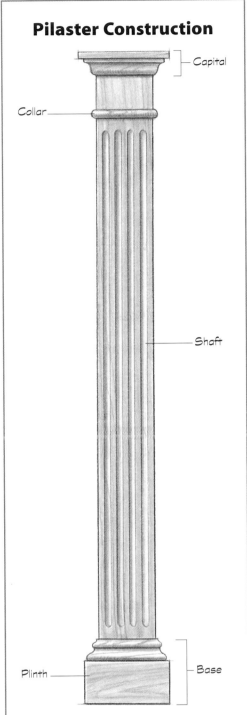

Pilaster Construction

Capital

Collar

Shaft

Plinth

Base

Two pilasters create an echo effect, opposite, in a fireplace wall: one adds vertical structure to the mantel, while the other defines the corner of the wall projection.

This striking pilaster, left, marks a grand stairway entrance. Actually two pilasters in one, they are carbon-copies of the door ornamentation.

Design Benefits. The design benefits of pilasters are numerous. With strong vertical lines, a projecting face, and a structural appearance, a pilaster is a highly visible ornament yet takes up very little space. These qualities make pilasters ideal for adding definition to wall openings and passageways. Pilasters can also divide spaces along a continuous wall plane. In many cases, pilasters offer relative subtlety in an application where a column would be obtrusive or seem excessive. And pilasters have an inherent "built-in" quality that makes them an appropriate decoration for many situations, adding a sense of craftsmanship to a home. Perhaps the most common locations for pilasters are alongside doorways and fireplace openings, visually supporting a header or mantelshelf above; they can be applied similarly as "supports" for countertops, shelves, ceiling cornices—virtually any horizontal plane or element.

MAKING YOUR OWN PILASTERS

The simple construction of pilasters makes building them a great project for do-it-yourselfers who don't mind a little design work and shopping around for the right molding. You can make the entire ornament with stock lumber and standard moldings. If you plan to paint the pilasters, use inexpensive pine or other softwood materials; for staining, use clear (knot-free) pine or hardwood. A quality lumberyard or specialty lumber dealer is a good place to begin shopping.

Plan the Top and Bottom. The widest parts of the pilaster will be the capital and the base, so plan them first to determine the overall width of the pilaster. Crown molding works well for capitals, which can be made more elaborate through a combination of cove, stop, baseboard, or other types of trim. For the base, select one or more moldings to finish the bottom of the shaft and cover the top edge of the plinth block. You can make the plinth from a single piece of wood or build it out with backing pieces and assemble the outer layer with three pieces of finish lumber mitered at the corners. If the pilaster runs from floor to ceiling, you might want to continue the room's baseboard around the plinth and have the capital tie into the room's crown molding or cornice.

Designing the Shaft. Create the shaft from a one-by knot-free board. If desired, mill flutes into the shaft face using a router with a core-box bit. Make sure the side edges of the board are straight and parallel before routing the flutes. Install the pieces to a wall using small amounts of construction adhesive and fastening to the wall framing with finishing nails. If there's no framing into which to nail, use hollow-wall anchors and finishing screws. For most projects, it's best to install the plinth block first, followed by the shaft, then cut the base and capital molding to fit around the shaft.

Stacked pilasters in this old fireplace mantel, left, bear some interesting hand-carved fluting.

Using the illusion of structure, tall pilasters, opposite, support a graceful relief element in this stunning composition of windows.

Room Dividers

One of the most common uses of columns and pilasters in the home is as part of a room divider. This purpose harkens back to their original uses in ancient buildings, where they supported arches and massive headers in grand passageways. Room dividers of all sorts have been popular architectural details ever since. In medieval-Gothic and early-Renaissance homes, adjoining spaces were divided by an arcade—a range of linked arches supported by columns. Later, these influenced Victorian builders, who created beautiful wood arcading with slender, turned columns and arches with ornate tracery or spindle work. The neoclassical interiors of Georgian, Federal, and Greek Revival homes were especially appropriate settings for classically styled room dividers, with pilaster-and-arch structures or columns supporting a header assembly suggestive of a stone entablature.

Column and Pedestal. One room divider that has remained a popular accent for modern interiors is the traditionally styled column-and-pedestal treatment. When applied to a standard, unadorned passageway, this treatment consists of short wing walls (the pedestals) on either side of the opening, each supporting a column that extends up to the header above the opening. (See "Building a Column & Pedestal Room Divider," opposite.) The header can be trimmed minimally, with a single band of door casing, or can receive an elaborate treatment with a frieze and cornice. The sides of the original opening should be trimmed as well. The framing of the pedestals is typically wrapped with a frame-and-panel finish or any decoration that blends with the neighboring wall treatments. If the original opening has no header, or soffit, coming down from the ceiling, you can install a false header before building the room divider. (See "Dressing Up a Passageway," on page 85.)

Design Advantages. This type of divider offers several advantages. The protruding pedestals and columns effectively separate adjoining spaces while retaining an open feeling and creating interesting views around the columns. Trim surrounding the original opening provides definition, adding architectural weight and serving as a frame for the entire treatment. For rooms with wainscoting, the pedestals provide a surface for extending the wall treatment into the opening to increase the sense of enclosure in the paneled room. Overall, the decorative effect of the divider is one of stateliness and elegance, making passage between rooms almost ceremonious.

A creative treatment of the column-and-pedestal room divider. Notable are the kinetic effect of the spiral columns and the stylized profiles above the capitals, suggestive of classical entablatures.

Building a Column & Pedestal Room Divider

To ensure that everything will fit properly, select the columns and all the trimwork before framing the pedestals. Build the pedestal frames with 2x6 lumber, and attach them to the side walls of the opening. For slim-

mer pedestals, you can rip the 2x6s down to match the width of the side walls. Sheath the pedestal frames with plywood; then add rails and stiles to create recessed panels. Install a shelf and molding to cap the pedestals, notching one end of the shelf to fit around the wall and create horns that extend beyond the trim.

Install one-by jambs under the header and at the sides of the opening. Make sure the columns will fit perfectly between the pedestal shelves and the header jamb. Install the columns so that their bases are aligned with the inside faces of the pedestals and the shelf ends overhang the bases.

Column & Pedestal Construction

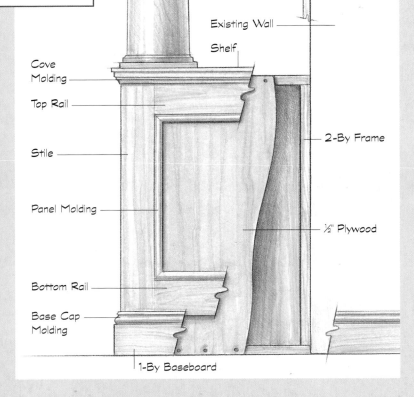

Header Assembly

Head Jamb

Column

Casing

Side Jamb

Existing Wall

Shelf

Cove Molding

Top Rail

Stile

Panel Molding

Bottom Rail

Base Cap Molding

2-By Frame

½" Plywood

1-By Baseboard

Buying Columns & Pilasters

Columns and pilasters are available primarily through architectural products dealers and specialty manufacturers. Price and materials vary, so it's a good idea to look at several offerings before buying. Columns are relatively expensive, and you'll want to make sure the quality of the details are satisfactory, lest you end up with something that looks too factory-made. Many suppliers and manufacturers of columns also carry pilasters, as well as pedestals, arches, corbels, brackets, and other related elements.

Best Selections. In general, companies that manufacture their own products offer the best selection of materials and custom options. Some, for example, will allow you to order half and three-quarter-columns for installing against a wall or over an outside corner, or they will split a whole column into sections to allow installation around a steel column or other structural member. For those who want authentically styled classical columns, a custom manufacturer is likely the only option. If you're willing to pay for it, some companies will even build totally custom pieces based on drawings you send them.

Recycled Columns. Another great way to get a unique ornament is to find one through an architectural salvage dealer. Considering that columns and pilasters are used for all types of buildings—from post offices to hotels to historical mansions—there's a good chance you'll find something of interest. And don't limit yourself to interior ornaments; salvaged exterior columns and pilasters are full of character earned from weathering the years.

Classically composed yet modern in design, opposite, a pair of columns and entablature frame an alcove for a kitchen range.

Decorative brackets, above, can add dimension and structure to pilasters.

In a casual sunroom, below, a classical half-column serves as a decorative counterpart to a brick column.

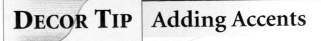

DECOR TIP | Adding Accents

Use an assortment of paint colors to accentuate the various details of bases, capitals, and flutes. Stencil column shafts with climbing vines or floral motifs. For a palatial effect, gild bases or capitals with gold paint.

CHAPTER 11

STAIRCASE DETAILS

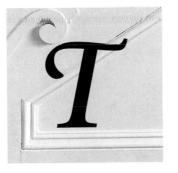

*T*he importance of the staircase to interior design is matched only by its practical service. Ascending at dramatic angles from floor to floor, traditional staircases proudly display fine materials and elegant, useful designs—appropriate as the first thing one sees from a home's entrance. When considered in parts, a staircase is full of architectural details, each contributing to the significant visual impact of the whole. While the balance between beauty and function has shifted toward the practical over the years, even the most ordinary modern staircases can be made over with a variety of upgrades and additions. The basic structure of most staircases (especially modern versions) allows for major decorative changes without rebuilding.

Anatomy of a Staircase

A notable characteristic of staircase design is that the finished product reveals very little about its basic construction. Without careful inspection, you can't see the supports and all the little joints and fasteners that hold the parts together. Identifying the standard parts and learning a little about how your staircase is built are the first steps to redecorating.

The supporting structure of a staircase is made up of two or more stringers, or carriages, typically 2×12 boards that span from floor to floor. The stringers either are cut in a sawtooth fashion and support the steps from below (known as a mitered stringer) or have grooves cut into

their side faces and support the steps from their ends (known as a housed stringer).

Treads and Risers. Each step of a staircase has two parts: the tread is the horizontal part that you walk on, and the riser is the vertical part between the treads. The tread and riser may be connected with dado (grooved) joints or may simply be butted together. With mitered stringers, the treads and risers are nailed in place; with housed stringers, their ends are secured within the stringer grooves by glued wedges. Some staircases also have a starting step, a wider, sometimes deeper first step that typically has one or more rounded ends and often supports the newel. (See below.)

Skirtboards. Where steps run along a wall, many staircases have a decorative skirtboard, which serves the same

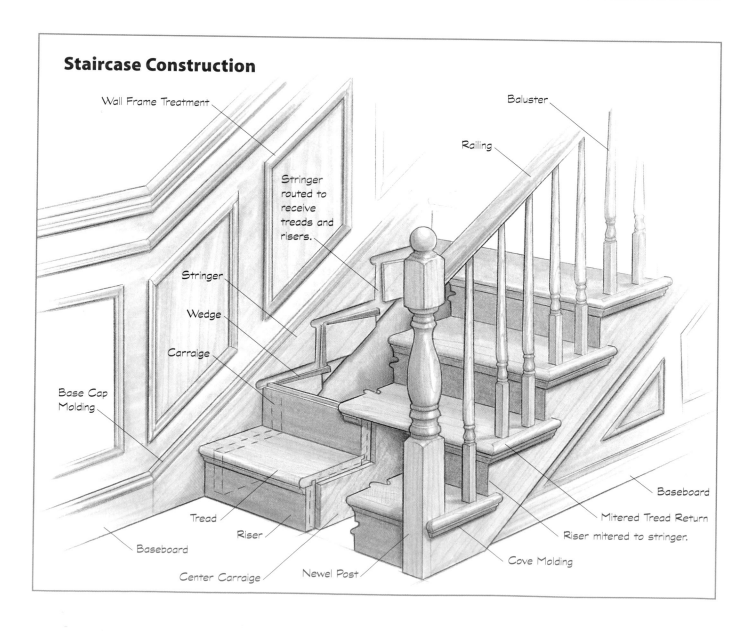

Staircase Construction

Wall Frame Treatment

Baluster

Railing

Stringer routed to receive treads and risers.

Stringer

Wedge

Carraige

Base Cap Molding

Tread

Riser

Baseboard

Center Carraige

Newel Post

Cove Molding

Baseboard

Mitered Tread Return

Riser mitered to stringer.

purpose as a baseboard. Modern staircase construction typically includes a continuous 2×4 spacer fixed between the stringer and the wall framing, providing a 1½-inch gap for installing drywall and in some cases, a skirtboard. If your stairs have no skirtboard, the gap between the stringer and wall makes it fairly easy to install one.

Balustrades. Staircase railing parts are known collectively as the balustrade, which includes the newels (or newel posts), the balusters, and the railing. Newels are the primary supports for the railing, while the balusters provide secondary support and create a barrier.

Traditional wood staircases with uncarpeted or partially carpeted steps are generally referred to as "finish" stairs, because their exposed parts have to be of finish quality. Steps intended to be fully carpeted are typically built with construction-grade materials.

STAIRCASE EVOLUTION

The fundamental design of the staircase has changed little over the years, but its architectural stardom has seen some ups and downs. Stairs in modest Colonial homes were often concealed behind a door in the fireplace wall. Late-Colonial and Georgian builders brought the staircase out into plain view in the central hallway. The prominent placement naturally led to more embellished decoration and a greater architectural significance for the staircase. Staircases in modern homes seem to follow the whim of the architect or the confines of the floor plan more than the tides of fashion.

A grand staircase, top, is often the first thing that meets people when they enter a house. The landing of this staircase has become a handy place to display art.

Grand historic homes often included decoration on the undersides of multistory staircases, center. This Craftsman-inspired design features trim bands along the undercarriage and landing newels with decorative pendants extending below the stair structure.

Steep, compact staircases, right, were common in Colonial homes, where they were often placed in unobtrusive locations. The fine balustrade details and applied trimwork are typical of late-period designs.

BUILDING CODES

The staircase is one of the most closely regulated elements of a house, and any changes that you make to yours must conform to the local building code. Everything from the steps to the stairwell width to the size and strength of the railing must meet strict specifications, and with good reason. Most of the time, stairs are climbed unconsciously—or blindly, when arms are full of laundry—and any irregularity, such as a shorter or longer step, or one with an excessive overhang, can cause a fall. Even if everyone in the home has gotten used to a known tricky spot, it will always be a hazard for guests. Most cosmetic changes won't require a permit, but it's a good idea to start your planning process by getting a copy of the staircase code from the local building department.

TREADS & RISERS

The treads and risers may be the most practical parts of a staircase, but they also have a significant impact on its appearance. Traditional finish stairs have polished hardwood treads and hardwood or paint-grade risers. If not left bare, they usually receive a carpet runner, a narrow strip of carpet with finished edges that leaves the attractive ends of the treads exposed. You can renew a worn set of finish stairs by adding a runner and refinishing the ends of the steps. One of the most dramatic staircase makeovers is turning a modern, carpeted version into a beautiful finish staircase by removing the carpet and adding new hardwood treads and riser panels. With some staircase configurations, you can also add an all-hardwood starting step to enhance the foot of the staircase.

TREAD & RISER MAKEOVERS

Replacing unfinished, construction-grade treads with hardwood is a good do-it-yourself project, but it's not for all types of staircases. It does not work with housed stringers, where the ends of the treads are seated in grooves and are too difficult to remove. Also, if the balusters rest on the treads, replacing the treads involves replacing or removing and reinstalling the balusters. Hardwood treads are available in one-piece versions for a full finished step, and in economical two-piece types made of particleboard with a specially cut end that receives a hardwood cap. The latter is used when you're also installing a carpet runner that will cover the particleboard. Commonly available hardwood species include oak, cherry, and maple, but others can be special-ordered. Some companies carry treads with wood-inlay decoration.

Riser Panels. An easy method for adding a finished look to risers is to cover them with ¼-inch-thick pieces of hardwood-veneer plywood or if you want to paint them, paint-grade plywood. Using thicker plywood is not recommended, as this will limit the tread depth too much. Traditional finish steps look best with a skirtboard, and this project presents a good opportunity for adding one.

TRIM TIP   Staircase Makeover

To add new treads and riser panels, carefully pry up the old treads. Measure and cut each riser panel individually; then test-fit each; finish as desired; and install with glue and finishing nails. Measure for each tread, and cut it to length. Test-fit the treads; then finish them as desired. Secure the treads to the stringers with adhesive and finishing nails driven through pilot holes. If desired, add scotia molding underneath the tread overhangs.

A fine, winding staircase, opposite, demonstrates the simple elegance of stained hardwood treads over painted risers.

Rich, contrasting finishes bring out the beauty of traditional stair parts, below left.

This charming staircase, below, features square-nosed oak treads, stenciled risers, and a simple, painted skirtboard. Slender balusters echo the spare newel detailing, and the railing is visually anchored at the wall by a square rosette.

STAIR RUNNERS

Carpet stair runners essentially offer the best of both worlds: the quiet, comfort, and sure footing of carpeted stairs and the natural wood beauty of finish stairs. Runners are traditional accents that add warmth and a finishing touch to bare wooden staircases. You can buy machine-made runners in the standard synthetic- and natural-fiber materials, specifying the length and width to fit your stairs.

Runner Installation. Installing a runner is not difficult with most staircases but does require carpet-laying tools. For comfort and to prevent wear, professional carpet installers recommend adding a firm, nonfoam pad at least ¼ inch thick applied over the top and nosing of each stair tread. Use tackless strips to secure the runner at the backs of the treads. For straight runs of stairs, you can install a runner in a single, continuous piece; winders (steps that turn a corner) require a specially cut piece for each step.

Stair Rods. These are a popular traditional embellishment for carpet runners. Available in various styles and metals, stair rods fit over the crease where each stair tread meets the bottom of the riser and are secured at the ends by decorative brackets. In the past, stair rods were used to hold carpet runners in place, but today they are purely ornamental.

STARTING STEPS

When added as an accent, a starting step is a finished hardwood step that replaces the first riser and tread of a mitered-stringer staircase. Starting steps are wider than regular steps—48 inches wide or more—and so create a kind of decorative platform suggestive of grand staircases that widen toward the bottom. They typically are rounded

Two hardwood starting steps, opposite left, give this enclosed staircase a more open, welcoming feel. The custom steps have square ends rather than the standard bull-nose.

A frame-and-panel wainscot with chair rail, opposite right, integrates this well-decorated stair-well into the surrounding decor.

An unusual feature, left, this bottom landing is framed by a grouping of newels with finials.

Carpet stair runners offer opportunities for creative decorating, below. Here, the playful scene displayed on each riser gains definition from a simple brass stair rod.

on their exposed end: if only one end is rounded (the other end abuts a wall), it's a single-bullnose step; if both ends are rounded, it's a double-bullnose. When a staircase has a newel, it is typically installed in the center of the starting step's bullnose end.

You can add a starting step as part of a tread replacement project; if there's no newel, it's like installing a new tread and riser at the same time. Incorporating a newel is fairly complicated, and you would probably need some professional help with the installation. Like treads, starting steps are available in various hardwood species and paint-grade materials, so you can match the other steps or choose a contrasting style for the starting step. One of the most elegant uses of a starting step is as a base for a scrolling volute newel.

DECOR TIP | Spiral Staircases

Spiral staircases have a romantic history, but in modern homes, building codes prohibit the use of spiral staircases as the only means of access between full stories. However, they can serve as secondary staircases between main levels or provide access to lofts and other private places. Factory-built spiral stairs are available in a variety of wood and metal designs, including complete, one-piece units and do-it-yourself assembly kits.

Balustrades

The balustrade is undoubtedly the most ornamental and visually dramatic part of a staircase. The eye delights in taking it all in: the stately newel, the graceful curves of the railing, the polished surfaces, the balusters in perfect repetition. Today, as in the past, a staircase balustrade is often the most ornate and finely crafted built-in feature of the home. The main balustrade elements (newels, railings, and balusters) are offered by stair parts manufacturers both separately and as sets. Common materials include hardwoods such as oak, maple, cherry, mahogany, and poplar (usually considered paint-grade because of its color variation), and iron and steel. Replacing any or all of the main parts can bring a dramatic change to your staircase. However, aside from replacing individual balusters, installing balustrade parts is not a job for amateurs.

NEWEL POSTS

Newels anchor the staircase railing and are the primary stylistic elements of the balustrade. They appear in an endless variety of styles, but the most common types available today are made of wood and are categorized as either "solid" or "box" type. Solid newels are just that—solid pieces of wood (although some are laminated) that are milled or turned on a lathe for a decorative profile. They are typically more slender than box types and often have square ends, a turned midsection, and an ornamental top. A volute newel is a traditional style consisting of a central solid newel supporting a scrolling railing end and surrounded by a column of balusters.

Box Newels. Box newels are hollow wood boxes topped with a molded wood cap and sometimes a finial ornament. The classic box is four-sided and may have embellishments such as flutes, chamfered corners, or levels of applied molding. Some newel designs combine a box-style base with a turned solid post. One interesting feature of box newels is their mounting hardware: traditional types are held in place with a long metal rod with threaded ends that extends from a plate affixed near the top of the newel down through the floor; nuts at either end of the rod are tightened to secure the post.

RAILINGS & BALUSTERS

Together, railings and balusters provide architectural definition to a staircase, in addition to their obvious functional roles. From a design standpoint, the two parts are related to the extent that the baluster's top end must conform to the hole or groove in the underside of the railing. Likewise, the bottom end of the baluster must fit with the tread or curb design. But beyond that, there's little that limits the decorative possibilities of a baluster or a railing and baluster combination.

Material Choices. Most railings are made of hardwood, but iron and steel are not uncommon. Railings are categorized as either over-the-post, which means the railing runs over the tops of the newels, or post-to-post, meaning the railing ends butt into the sides of the newels. The differences are primarily aesthetic, although with post-to-post railings you have to remove your hand from the railing at transitions. Where railing ends do not meet newels, decorative options include curved or mitered wall returns, decorative blocks called rosettes that receive the railing end at a wall, and half newels—a partial newel installed flush to a wall.

Balusters. Installing most balusters is fairly straightforward but does require careful cutting and measuring. Balusters with rounded top ends fit into holes in the underside of the railing, while square-top styles are nailed into a groove and have thin wood plates, called fillets, applied between the balusters. Most wood balusters have square bottom ends and attach to the treads or to a low curb with nails or by means of a dowel or tenon that fits into a hole in the tread. Some treads have a little piece of applied nosing trim covering the dowel or tenon. New baluster blanks have elongated top ends that you cut to match the slope of the railing.

The advent of household electricity inspired some architects to incorporate light fixtures into their newel designs, above right.

The combination of wood and metal is a popular treatment for custom balustrades, right. This modified volute-style newel employs a deep starting step.

Staircase Accents

In addition to upgrading its essential parts, you can enhance the appearance of a staircase with a number of applied features that can be added without altering the basic staircase parts.

SKIRTBOARDS & TREAD BRACKETS

Skirtboards can be added to unfinished basement or attic staircases and to carpeted stairs that have gaps between the rough tread and the wall. In these applications, the installation involves cutting the ends of the skirtboard to follow the top riser and the floor at the foot of the staircase and slipping the board between the treads and the wall. Without the gap at the wall, you would face the monumental task of making a cutout for each step.

Skirtboards come in standard dimensions of $^{11}/_{16} \times 11$

TRIM TIP   Finding Stair Parts

You can find a limited selection of the main parts at home centers and lumberyards, but stair parts manufacturers carry a larger selection. Other sources include millwork companies and architectural products dealers. You can also find some parts, such as newels and various accessories, at salvage yards and antique shops.

inches, in 8-, 10-, 14-, and 16-foot lengths. They usually are made of particleboard with a hardwood veneer. Architecturally, a skirtboard performs the same role as a baseboard. At the bottom and top of the stairs, the skirtboard should be joined by a matching baseboard or terminated at a decorative transition block that abuts the baseboard.

Tread Brackets. A good way to embellish the ends of treads on the open side of a staircase is to install tread brackets. They were especially popular accents in Georgian and later Colonial homes, but are found in all styles of historic homes. These purely decorative details are very easy to install, requiring a little glue and a few small finishing nails to keep them in place.

STAIR SEATS

Stair seats are built-in features that were born out of the custom of placing furniture, such as a bench or settle, against the wall next to the bottom of a staircase. They are found in Colonial-style homes, country farmhouses, and some Victorian homes, but they were favorite details of Craftsman-style designers, who liked the stair seat for its practical use of space. More importantly, the built-in seat promoted the concept of turning hallways and staircases into living spaces rather than service areas.

In design, stair seats are similar to window seats. Corners and alcoves created by L-shaped stairs are ideal locations, but you can add a stair seat under any open-sided staircase. Like window seats, a stair seat can be made with a flip-up lid concealing a handy storage space.

Tread brackets, opposite top, traditionally concealed the exposed ends of stair risers. These historic examples are enhanced further by a thin band of decorative ogee molding.

Used as a decorative shelf, this traditional stair seat, opposite bottom, dresses up an entryway. This feature works well in traditional and Craftsman-style homes.

A shadow railing with half newels, above, is a classic molding treatment. Here it creates a striking profile against a stark white background.

Shadow Railings. A novel variation of the paneling treatment involves using trim to create a "shadow railing" on the staircase wall. A shadow railing is not a functional railing, but merely projecting trimwork that mirrors the lines of the balustrade railing. A popular decoration in Georgian and some Colonial homes, shadow railings were often enhanced with half newels placed at the appropriate locations. Their decorative effect is an interesting combination of formal and playful characteristics, and they add a strong linear element that increases the visual impact of the staircase.

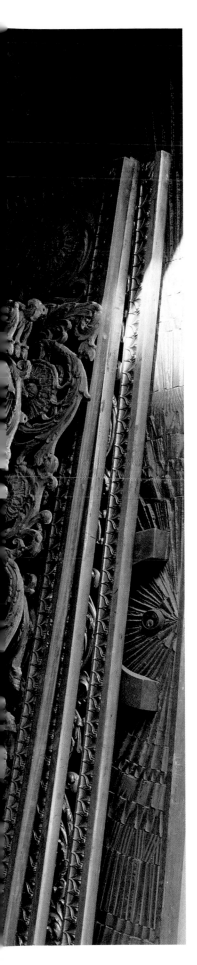

CHAPTER 12

ARCHITECTURAL SALVAGE

While most architectural ornaments are based on designs and styles from the past, architectural salvage is the past. A salvage warehouse is a jungle of domestic relics: mantels, bathtubs, chimney pots, doorknobs, garden urns, iron gates, columns, balusters—pieces that provide their own inspiration and tell their own stories. Since the late 1960s, the growing salvage market has been a source as much for restorers of historic homes as for average homeowners seeking novelties and unique art pieces. Quality salvage items are not inexpensive; they are valued as antique artifacts that display a craftsmanship and use of materials rarely found in modern products. If you're doing any kind of decorating or remodeling, it's worth taking a trip to a local salvage dealer.

Salvage Outlets

Places to find architectural salvage cover a fairly broad range, from high-end boutiques to job-site dumpsters. Over the last two decades, growth in the salvage trend has caused a steady rise in prices, while salvage businesses have moved toward more upscale presentation and pricier merchandise. But the greater demand for old goods has also increased the supply, meaning more people are saving and reselling rather than throwing away. As a result, more architectural ornaments are appearing in low-end retail outlets such as thrift stores and flea markets. Meanwhile, the Internet has expanded its role in the salvage market, linking people to dealers across the country and around the world.

ARCHITECTURAL DEALERS

The best place to search for salvage is at a bona fide architectural warehouse. These are run by people who know the business and have a real love of quality "junk." Establishments on the no-frills end are dusty buildings with stuff strewn everywhere; at the high end, businesses appeal to expensive clientele with artistic displays of salvage items in home-like settings.

Dealers who know their stuff are the best to buy from. Often they can tell you about the origins of the pieces they

sell and can give tips on period decorating, working with different materials, and even using pieces in unconventional ways. Some dealers offer a search service and will track down a specific item for you.

Locating Dealers. Most sizable cities have at least one or two salvage dealers—look in the phone book under "Salvage," "Antiques," and "Demolition Contractors." You can also search for, and even shop from, out-of-state dealers over the Internet. One advantage of visiting a local shop is that it will carry historic items from your area.

ANTIQUE SHOPS

It's only natural that some salvage pieces would show up in antique shops. Most antiques dealers carry small items such as mirrors, decorative shelves, and lamps, but some collect building parts and may have a set of old porch columns stashed out back. Check antique furniture shops for reclaimed built-ins and glass specialists for stained glass windows. Some dealers advertise that they sell "architectural antiques," a commonly used name for architectural salvage.

An old column finds a new home, opposite top, bringing with it a touch of splendor from its former life.

Consider using salvaged finds in unusual ways. This wall hanging, opposite bottom, is actually an old gable-end louver.

Here's a decorative use for an old window frame, left. It adds old-fashioned charm to a modern setting. Note how its design mimics the larger window.

Some architectural dealers specialize in carrying pieces for all aspects of interior design, including furniture and artwork, below.

SMART TIP | Go Digital

Because digital cameras provide instant images that you can save and review later, they are great for salvage shopping. Take one along if you are trying to find a piece that completes a set or fills a particular spot in your home.

BUDGET SALVAGE

There are a few different types of outlets that may carry a limited selection of salvaged details, most of which are priced lower than architectural dealers' prices. Large thrift stores with home products sometimes have salvaged ornaments. Ornaments also turn up at flea markets, amid the vast array of new and used miscellanies. Auctions are other possibilities—check the newspaper for announcements. Historic preservation offices sometimes run small salvage yards. It's also possible that your city offers items claimed from local commercial buildings.

INTERNET SHOPPING

Many well-established architectural dealers have their own Web sites on which you can browse their latest stock. Some businesses offer online buying, while others prefer that you come in and see the real thing (or at least call them) before buying. In any case, the Web is a good source for seeing what's out there without having to leave home. You can even tap into markets abroad for a look at European salvage offerings.

Focusing on salvage, right, a fireplace features reclaimed shutters, an old Federal mantel, and a weathered fanlight decoration.

Don't forget to rummage outside, opposite top. Outdoor salvage yards are full of iron doors, gates, and balconies; reclaimed timbers and lumber; and garden ornaments.

Items that appear unconnected in a salvage yard may work well together in an interior setting, opposite bottom.

Shopping Tips

Browsing for architectural salvage requires nothing more than an open mind and perhaps a curious nature. However, if you're looking for a piece to serve a specific purpose or fill a particular space, make note of all the facts before leaving home. Record the dimensions of related pieces or sizes of spaces, think about color and materials you might like or dislike, and if possible, take photographs for visual reference. If you're trying to match an item at home or find a missing piece to go with an existing set, bring the parts with you—it will make it much easier to identify a match and give the dealer something from which to work.

Be Prepared. In addition to your notes, a few tools can help get you one step closer to making a decision. A tape measure and a pad of paper and pencil allow you to record specifics about items you find, so you won't have to rely on memory when you get back home. A magnet comes in handy for investigating metalwork. Magnets are

attracted to any metal that contains iron, which makes it highly prone to rust (not necessarily a bad thing when it comes to salvage).

Bringing tools and reference items helps prepare you for one of the most important aspects of salvage shopping: making a decision. While some minor salvage items may be a dime a dozen, better pieces are often one-of-a-kind, and you can't order replacements once they're gone. Unless the owner will hold an item for you, you're taking a risk by leaving the store without it. Quick turnover in a store also means that new items are flowing through at a regular rate, so it pays to visit often.

Check Catalogs. If you're decorating within a particular style or period, old building materials catalogs can be a great resource. Full of illustrated details of doors, windows, mantels, trimwork, and stair parts, period catalogs may be reprinted versions from the actual time of the period or restoration manuals for old-home buffs. You can find them at the library and bookstores, and architectural salvage dealers often have their own copies.

BUILDING CODES

Old decorations add charm to a home, but some can actually break the law. The problem is that many old fixtures and mechanical items don't meet today's building codes. If you plan to use a salvaged mantel to decorate a real fireplace (instead of using it as a headboard, for instance), make sure the mantel's opening meets the local fire code.

Code Violators. Bathtubs, toilets, and electrical fixtures are other common code violators. Salvage dealers often rewire old lamps to sell them as working pieces, but if a fixture has worn or outdated wiring, it's worth the few dollars for replacement parts so you don't bring home something that can burn the house down. Building inspectors don't usually make house calls to people who aren't on their permit list, so you'll have to rely on common sense when putting salvage pieces to use. If you're remodeling and your house is on the list, be forewarned that inspectors can be picky about refurbished fixtures and details.

SMART TIP | Wax On, Wax Off

Don't assume every old piece needs to be stripped down to the bare wood. Sometimes years of wax and grime hide a perfectly good finish. Clean items with mineral spirits (test in an inconspicuous spot) before deciding to totally refinish.

A cleaned up old window sash, right, takes its place in a modern setting.

A salvaged iron chair, part of a hand-painted sign, and other accessories combine with old garden items to create a unique design theme, opposite top.

A reclaimed eyebrow window above the bed, opposite bottom, contributes to the Early American decor of this bedroom. Note that the frame was left distressed rather than refinished.

Buying & Reclaiming Materials

Salvage items come in all types of traditional materials and in various states of preservation (or decay). After years of weathering or repainting, it's not always easy to identify a material or its condition. Some pieces require a fair amount of work to reclaim them from an unsightly state, but many look good just as they are, full of age and character. Following are some tips to help you assess items before buying, as well as suggestions for working with old materials. If the refurbishing work seems beyond your ability, ask the salvage dealer to recommend local restoration professionals. When doing the work yourself, be aware that most old paint contains lead, so be sure to take the necessary precautions to avoid inhaling or ingesting paint particles while stripping or refinishing.

WOOD

Wood pieces in decent condition can generally be refinished like furniture. When shopping, always check for rot, and be realistic about the condition of painted wood—don't assume that it will look perfect when stripped. Rough timbers and salvaged lumber often need a serious cleaning, which you can do with a pressure washer or a wire brush. Treat all lumber for rot, insects, and fungus before building with it; otherwise the problem could affect neighboring wood members.

SMART TIP   Test the Finish

Apply a dab of fingernail polish remover in a hidden spot on your salvaged item. If the finish softens, it is lacquer, shellac, or varnish. Use a refinishing product on these pieces. If the finish does not soften, it is probably polyurethane. Use a paint stripper to remove this finish.

Awaiting a buyer, above, an old European stove shares space with iron openwork screens and a glazed plaque. Check metal items for rust before purchasing.

An antique cabinet with hand-painted panels, above right, fits in well with modern cabinetry. Refurbishing the piece would have ruined its unique look.

A salvaged marble fireplace mantel, opposite, enhances an otherwise drab brick fireplace. When buying reclaimed mantels, be sure they comply with local fire codes.

Stripping Methods. For stripping painted wood, you have a few options. Sanding is the simplest method but also the most time-consuming and can be difficult in detailed areas. Stripping with a heat gun can be effective, but it's not recommended for an inexperienced hand, as it's easy to scorch the wood. Chemical stripping is usually the best option for fine details and textured work—it's messy and toxic, but it's effective. You can also have a professional dip the piece in a vat of caustic solution, which

METAL

Good, old-fashioned metal parts make great salvage finds, and there are several methods for bringing new life to worn, rusty pieces. When shopping for iron and steel, look for quality in the clarity of detail work. Older cast-iron pieces, such as urns and statuary, tend to be of higher quality than newer versions. Welded iron usually indicates the piece was made after 1920.

Removing Rust. To remove rust, use a hand held wire brush or a rotary attachment on a power drill, or you can have the piece sandblasted at an auto body shop. Once you're down to bare, polished metal, you can coat it with clear furniture wax or lacquer, or paint it with a high-quality spray paint. For an old-time blackened finish, treat iron with stove blackening paste, which also serves as a protectant. Other metals, such as brass, copper, and zinc, can be cleaned and shined with an appropriate polish. Chrome fittings and hardware are often brass underneath chrome plating—these can be stripped or refinished by professionals.

works only on oil-based (alkyd) paints. The dipping method is convenient but the process can be damaging to hardwoods and glued joints and may discolor the wood.

Before stripping any wood item, make sure none of the piece is made of composition (or "compo") material—a mixture of wood pulp and glue often used to create molded details on mantels and other ornaments. Composition work can be damaged by standard paint strippers and should be handled by a professional.

GLASS

Stained glass windows are among the most sought-after salvage items, but they can be expensive to repair. Professional stained glass restorers can remedy most problems, but you might want to get an estimate before buying a window that you plan to have fixed. To asses a stained glass piece, inspect the cames (the metal channels securing the glass) and their solder joints for damage. Most cames are lead, while some are made of harder metals and have joints that make glass replacement difficult; in some cases, getting to a single piece requires disassembling the whole framework. Also inspect the glass for cracks and a whitish film, called chalking, which is a permanent condition that goes away only temporarily when the glass is wet.

STONE & TERRA-COTTA

Stone, terra-cotta, marble, and concrete artifacts are usually salvaged in good condition, because these types of pieces lose much of their value when key elements are severely cracked or missing. This doesn't mean you should expect perfection. Minor cracks, weathered details, paint and stains, and clinging bits of old mortar are common but generally don't mar the appearance much. You can remove unwanted mortar and brick pieces—very carefully—with a masonry chisel. A good scrubbing with soap and water removes old dirt and grime. Removing paint from these materials generally doesn't work well, as the porous surfaces retain the coloring. Stone and masonry items can be very heavy, and you'll need to take special care when moving them, lest a nose gets chipped or an arm broken.

SMART TIP | Reproductions

If you can't find what you're looking for in the world of salvage, check out the reproduction market. Better reproduction works are modeled after actual old pieces, offering authentic design and brand-new condition.

Salvaged implements from a farm auction make great details for a Country interior, opposite.

A shop full of stained glass, left, is an enchanting place to browse and admire the beauty of traditional craftsmanship.

A fan-shaped ornament from the exterior of a house in Maine, below left, decorates this modern interior living room.

Found hand-painted tiles provide just the right accent for this master bathroom, below.

CHAPTER 13

TOOLS, MATERIALS & TECHNIQUES

*W*hile many architectural details are in the form of easy-to-install products, few projects can be completed without some use of tools and basic building materials. Of course, custom projects involve even more work, but they also offer the added rewards of unique designs and a sense of personal accomplishment. Whatever your decorating goals are, it helps to become familiar with the basic tools, materials, and building techniques used for most home projects. The basics shown here are standards for professionals and amateurs alike. A primer on power tools is included for those who may not yet own all the "essentials"—the cutting and fastening tools that get used again and again because they simplify the most fundamental building tasks.

Power Tools

Do-it-yourselfers own more power tools now than ever before, and with good reason. Most power tools not only make the work go faster than their equivalent hand tools, they also require less skill to be used accurately. The basic tool collection shown here is sufficient to complete most decorative building and finishing projects in your home. All of these tools are commonly available for rent at a rental center, which is a good option for finishing a critical phase of a project without having to purchase the tool.

MITER SAWS

A miter saw is the ultimate trim tool because it allows you to make perfect cuts in a full range of angles. It's also incredibly efficient for making identical cuts in multiple pieces. The alternative to a power miter saw is a hand miter box, and if you're installing more than a few pieces of trim, it will be worth it to rent a power saw for the job. There are three types of miter saws: standard, compound, and sliding compound.

Standard saws have blades that are fixed in a vertical position and can pivot—both left and right—to make cuts from 0 degrees (square cut) to 45 degrees. These saws can handle the majority of cuts needed for basic trimwork.

Compound Miter Saws. Compound miter saws pivot just like standard saws, but their blade housings can also be tilted sideways to make bevel cuts from 0 to 45 degrees. This enables the saw to make compound cuts—simultaneously making an angled cut across the face of a board and a bevel cut along its end grain. Compound cuts are

Compound miter saws cut angles and bevels in one pass (sliding model shown).

required when joining two trim boards that lie on different planes, or when making any cut on crown molding. Compound saws enable you to cut crown molding with the molding lying flat on the saw table.

Sliding Compound Miter Saws. Sliding compound saws not only pivot and tilt, but also slide forward and backward, increasing their cutting capacity significantly over the other saw types. For example, a sliding saw with a standard 8-inch blade can make a straight cut through a 1×12 board, a cut you would normally have to make with a circular saw. Sliding miter saws are quite pricey and really offer more capacity than most homeowners need.

An important consideration for any type of miter saw is blade size, which relates directly to cutting capacity. Small saws with 7¼-inch blades are somewhat lighter, and thus more portable, than 10- or 12-inch models, but they have more limited cutting ability. A good option is a compound miter saw with a 10-inch blade.

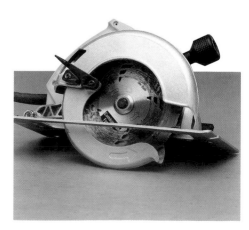

Circular saws have an adjustable table that rotates for different cutting depths and tilts for bevel cuts.

A jigsaw with variable speed control makes it easy to freehand curves, cutouts, and specialty detail cuts.

Making a Plywood Cutting Jig

A cutting jig allows you to make long, straight cuts in lumber and sheet materials, helping your circular saw work more like a table saw. To make the jig, snap a chalk line lengthwise across a 12-inch-wide piece of ½- or ¾-inch plywood. Fasten a straight 1x4 guide board to the plywood with screws, using the chalk line to ensure that the guide board is straight. Carefully cut off the edge of the plywood by running a circular saw with its table along the guide board. To use the jig, align the cut plywood edge with the cutting line on your workpiece. Make the cut with the saw base sliding smoothly along the guide board.

13

Cutting Jig Construction

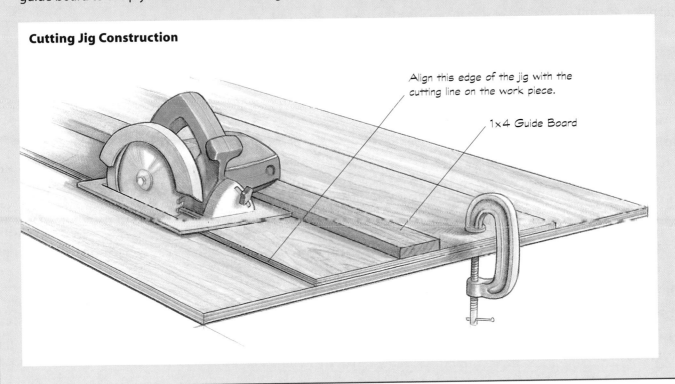

Align this edge of the jig with the cutting line on the work piece.

1x4 Guide Board

CIRCULAR SAWS

Next to the drill, the circular saw is the most versatile power tool available. It can cut virtually any material (including masonry, with the proper blade) and is highly portable yet powerful. All circular saws make square cuts and a full range of bevel cuts up to 45 degrees. In fact, the main limitation of a circular saw is the user—most people find it difficult to make perfectly straight cuts with a circular saw. A simple remedy for this is to use a straightedge as a cutting guide. For quick, straight crosscuts in lumber and pieces up to 12 inches wide or so, use a Speed Square as a straightedge: hold the lip of the square tight against the board's edge, and run the saw base along the perpendicular edge of the square. For long rip cuts, use a cutting jig. (See "Making a Plywood Cutting Jig," above.)

JIGSAWS

Also called saber saws, jigsaws make curved cuts in wood and other materials. They have a single reciprocating blade that moves straight up and down and a saw base that tilts for making bevel cuts. Jigsaws also enable you to make cutouts within a workpiece. To do this, first drill a starter hole just inside the cutout outline. Insert the jigsaw blade into the hole to begin the cut. Most jigsaw styles are similar, but variable speed control is an important feature. It's also important to use the proper blade for the job.

DRILLS

The innovation of the keyless chuck has made the drill one of the handiest household tools. This feature allows you to change from a drill bit to a screwdriver bit quickly. Standard drills are ⅜ inch, which refers to the maximum bit-shaft diameter the drill can accept. Cordless drills offer great convenience over regular corded models, but there are some tradeoffs between the two. On average, corded drills are faster and more responsive, provide more consistent power than cordless models, and are much less expensive. Essential features for either type include a keyless chuck, reversible drive, and variable speed control. Topping the list of best accessories are: a magnetic bit holder/driver, a clutch driver for screwing in drywall, and a combination piloting/countersink bit.

ROUTERS

Routers are powerful rotary tools that use interchangeable bits to make a variety of cuts and details. In a home workshop, they're used most commonly to round over or sculpt the edges of boards, cut grooves for making traditional woodworking joints, and carve decorative details into the faces of wood pieces. When set up in a simple router table, a router can be used to mill custom molding and other trim pieces. Standard routers have a fixed depth adjustment that must be set before use. Plunge routers can

The more molding a room contains, the more it makes sense to buy or rent a pneumatic nailer. This room alone contains extensive window casing, picture rail molding, crown, and base molding.

Using a Pneumatic Nailer

If you rent a nailer, make sure the sales assistant explains the basics of setting up the equipment, running the compressor, safety issues, etc. To use a nailer, load a full nail clip into the magazine. Point the gun away from you at all times. Most nailers have a spring-loaded safety mechanism in the tip that prevents the gun from firing unless the tip is depressed, but a misfire is not uncommon. Position the gun perpendicular to the workpiece; press the tip firmly against the surface; and pull the trigger to fire the nail.

Avoid driving nails into wood knots, which can bend the nail or cause the knot to blow apart. Also, always keep your free hand several inches away from

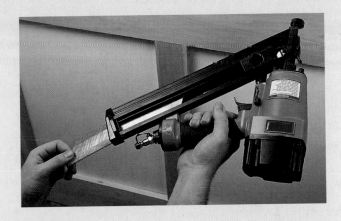

the nailing point—if a fired nail hits an obstacle, like a screw or framing nailhead, it's end can curl back and out through the top or side of the workpiece.

move freely up and down on their bases, enabling the user to plunge the bit into the material at any point. Router bits come with shaft diameters of ¼ and ½ inch. For most home projects, ¼-inch bits are suitable (and are often much less expensive). Routers may be designed for ¼- or ½-inch bits, but ½-inch models usually include an extra collet that accepts the smaller bit shaft.

Routers are made more versatile and useful with a good selection of bits and a detachable guide fence for making straight cuts.

PNEUMATIC NAILERS

Pneumatic nailers are air-powered guns used for fastening lumber and trimwork. Not many do-it-yourselfers own them, but renting a nail gun is money well spent for large trim projects. Nailers offer several advantages over traditional hammer-and-nail fastening: the gun holds a clip of dozens of nails that can be fired semiautomatically without reloading; you can operate the tool with one hand, leaving the other hand free to hold the workpiece; and the nails go in so easily that there's almost none of the violent banging and vibrating associated with hammering. Another advantage is that nailers automatically countersink the nails and omit the need for pilot holes.

Brad nailers (below) and **finish nailers** (right) are lightweight and easy to operate with one hand. The nailer must be used only with compatible nail clips.

Materials

Modern construction materials are produced and designed for economy and longevity. And while it's true that the quality of lumber isn't what it used to be, engineered products continue to get better, in terms of both quality and ease of application. So while a homeowner in the 1920s was able to build bookshelves using solid oak boards, a remodeler of the same home today can use oak-veneer plywood, and no one is the wiser.

CONSTRUCTION LUMBER

Construction lumber describes the structural-grade one-by boards and two-by framing lumber used for general building work. Construction-grade one-by boards are classified as "common" and usually have knots and other imperfections. Framing lumber, also called dimension lumber, is classified by its strength, based on the wood species and general condition.

FINISH LUMBER

Finish lumber refers to finish-grade one-by boards that look good enough to be stained or clear-finished and includes quality softwoods and hardwoods of all types.

SMART TIP   The Cutoff Bin

For small projects, you can save money by buying partial sheets of plywood or MDF from the cutoff bin at lumberyards and home centers. Also, 4 x 4-foot half-sheets are also commonly available at reduced prices.

Paint-grade finish lumber is high-quality lumber but may have inconsistent coloring or uninteresting grain patterns. Poplar, aspen, and some pines are common paint-grade lumber species. At a lumberyard, finish lumber may be classified as any one of a number of "select" grades, perhaps including a "clear" grade, which implies that the boards are knot-free. Inspect the material carefully before buying, making sure boards are flat, straight, and unblemished. Standard lumberyards carry some selection of hardwood finish lumber, home centers also carry a selection of the most popular species, while specialty yards and dealers offer greater selections of wood species and lumber dimensions.

Typical Shelving Materials

Pine

Plywood

Hardwood

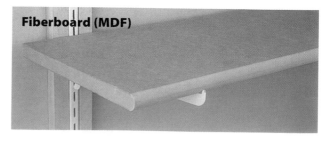
Fiberboard (MDF)

PLYWOOD & MDF

Plywood is arguably the best all-around building material. It's strong and stable (meaning it resists warping); it holds fasteners well; and it has perfectly consistent dimensions. As a finish material, plywood is much less expensive than solid-wood boards. Plywood comes in standard thicknesses of ¼-, ⅜-, ½-, ⅝-, ¾-, and 1-inch, in 4×8-foot sheets or special-order 4×10-foot sheets.

Standard plywood is made with layers of softwood and comes in several grades for interior work. A-B grade is smooth and attractive on both sides, but one side looks slightly better than the other.

Best Grades. Cabinet-grade is the highest-quality plywood. It's made with hardwood layers and is attractive on both sides. The hardwood layers also make the panel's edges more attractive and free of voids.

Both standard and cabinet-grade plywood is available with outer veneers of many different hardwood species. Oak, birch, and mahogany are the most common, but a good lumberyard may offer maple, cherry, walnut, and other varieties. These are generally referred to by name, such as "oak-veneer" or "birch-veneer." A word of warning: hardwood veneers on plywood are highly prone to splintering when cut with a saw, especially when cut across the grain. To minimize this problem, use a sharp saw blade and a straightedge, and score the veneer along the cutting line.

Like Real Wood. MDF is the abbreviated (and common) name for *medium-density fiberboard*. It's made from wood fibers bonded with glue and is primarily used as a plywood alternative for cabinets and finish work. Standard MDF must be painted, but there are also types with hardwood veneers made for staining. MDF is easy to cut, rout, and sand, and it takes paint better than plywood. The disadvantages are that it's heavy, and the bare material is prone to swelling when wet; seal edges before painting.

DRYWALL

Drywall sheets come in thicknesses of ¼-, ⅜-, ½-, ⅝-, ¾-inch in 4-foot widths and in lengths ranging from 8 to 16 feet. Standard ½-inch panels are used for most wall, ceilings, and soffits. Thinner panels work well for covering over old, damaged drywall.

Joints are filled with drywall compound and reinforcing tape. For most projects, all-purpose joint compound is the easiest and most convenient to use. It comes premixed in plastic tubs.

For Corners. Corners require special treatment. Inside corners are reinforced with a tape that creases down the center. Outside corners are covered with a metal or paper-flanged bead. There is also a flexible bead for finishing curved surfaces.

Finish shelving with a decorative edge treatment. You can apply nosing to plywood or solid wood shelves, or you can use a router to create a unique edge treatment when using solid-wood shelves.

Techniques

Many of the special techniques required for adding architectural details involve cutting and installing trim. Crown molding in particular can be tricky if you're not familiar with the basic installation methods. Whether you're nailing up trim, securing bookcases, or hanging a shelf, you'll face the sometimes mystifying task of finding wall studs or ceiling joists—but this is not difficult once you understand the layout of standard framing. If there's no framing where you need it, you can attach the material using hollow-wall anchors. Projects that involve drywall shouldn't be daunting either. The process may be time-consuming, but the techniques are straightforward.

CUTTING CROWN MOLDING

Because crown molding is "sprung," or sits at an angle to the wall and ceiling surfaces, all cuts made to join pieces at corners are compound cuts. The proper technique for cutting crown molding depends on the type of miter saw you're using. Outside corners require miter joints, while inside corners look best with coped joints.

Standard Miter Saw or Hand Miter Box. The trick to cutting miters with a standard saw is to place the molding upside down and backwards on the saw table. Think of the horizontal saw table as the ceiling and the vertical saw fence as the wall. Hold the molding at an angle so the flat edges on the back side (those that contact the ceiling and wall) are flat against the saw table and fence. Make the cut with the saw set at 45 degrees.

Although it usually appears at the top of a wall, crown molding, above, can also add distinction to cabinetry and built-ins.

Crown molding sits at an angle to the wall, opposite. This makes installation a little tricky for someone not used to working with the material.

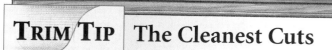

TRIM TIP | The Cleanest Cuts

There are a variety of different type blades available for your miter saw. The blade packaging usually describes how the blade should be used, but in general, blades with more teeth and carbide tips produce the cleanest cuts.

Compound Miter Saw. A compound miter saw makes an angled cut and a beveled cut in one pass. This allows you to cut with the molding laid flat on the saw table, so visualizing the cuts is easier than when working with a basic miter saw. The first step is determining the angle at which the wide middle portion of the molding's back side meets the wall. Most are angled at 45 degrees or 52 degrees.

For 45-degree molding, rotate the saw to cut a 35.3 degree angle, and tilt the saw to cut a 30-degree bevel. For 52-degree molding, set the saw angle at 31.6 degrees and the bevel at 33.9. (Check your saw's instructions.)

Basic versus Compound Miter Saws

Basic miter saw is shown cutting an inside corner for coping the left-side piece. The molding is bottom up on the saw's table.

Compound miter saw is shown cutting the inside corner for coping the left-side piece. The molding lies flat; the top edge is against the saw fence.

MITERED RETURNS

Sometimes a piece of molding stops short of a wall corner or doesn't meet with an adjoining molding, and its end requires a special treatment for a finished look. One option is to bevel-cut a portion of the end and add a mitered return. (See "Making Mitered Returns," right.)

MAKING A COPED JOINT

A coped joint is made with one piece of molding that is square-cut and butted into an inside corner and a second, perpendicular, piece that is cut with a coping saw to match the profile on the face of the first piece. Coped joints work better than miter joints on inside corners because they don't spread apart when nailed, like miters do, and they tend to gap less if the wood molding shrinks.

After you've installed the square-cut piece, make an inside corner miter cut on the section that will be coped. This cut exposes the end grain and makes a clean edge for making the coped cut. Using a coping saw, carefully cut along the profiled edge of the face of the molding.

HAND-NAILING TRIM

When hand nailing, wood trim and other finish details may be prone to splitting, especially near the ends of a piece. To prevent splitting, drill pilot holes for the nails, using a drill bit that is equal to or slightly smaller than the nail shaft diameter. Hardwood trim usually requires pilot holes for all nails. After recessing, or setting, the nails, fill the nailholes with putty and sand the surface smooth before painting or staining.

To create a coped joint, hold the coping saw at about a 30-degree angle to the molding face, back-cutting the end grain material along the profile, above right.

Drive nails through the pilot holes, stopping when the nailhead is about $\frac{1}{8}$ in. from the wood surface, right. Using a nail set with a point that is slightly smaller than the nailhead, drive the nail about $\frac{1}{16}$ in. below the surface.

Installing trim in a typical room, opposite, requires the expertise to make a variety of specialty cuts and use a variety of tools. The installer needs patience and the ability to pay careful attention to small details.

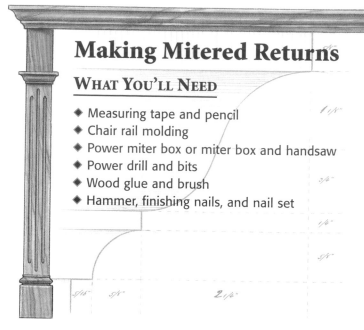

Making Mitered Returns

WHAT YOU'LL NEED

◆ Measuring tape and pencil
◆ Chair rail molding
◆ Power miter box or miter box and handsaw
◆ Power drill and bits
◆ Wood glue and brush
◆ Hammer, finishing nails, and nail set

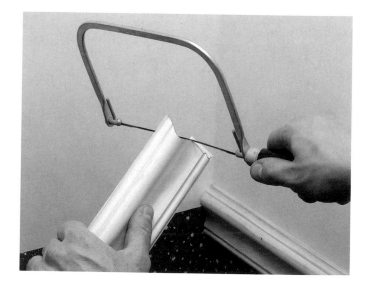

1 If trim stops short of a corner, finish the edge with a mitered return. Cut the molding end at 45 degrees and install it, using finishing nails. Cut it so that the mitered edge faces the wall.

2 Using a scrap piece of molding, miter-cut the end at 45 degrees in the direction opposite to the installed piece. Make a second, square cut to create a triangular return. Glue the return piece to the end of the installed molding.

13

Tools, Materials & Techniques

Installing a Wall Niche

WHAT YOU'LL NEED

- Foam niche, template, and tape
- Pencil and utility saw
- Caulking gun and construction adhesive
- Hammer and 8d finishing nails
- Pencil
- Nail filler

1 A niche usually comes with a template that you can tape to the wall and use as a cutting guide.

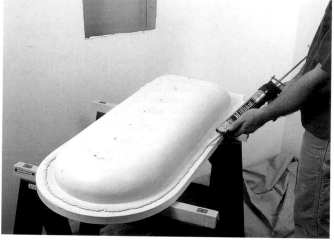

2 A foam-formed niche has a flange to which you apply adhesive to adhere the unit to the wall.

3 Press the unit into place; secure it with a few finishing nails into adjacent studs; and touch up the nailholes.

FORMING SPECIAL OPENINGS

Adding some decorative details, such as installing a wall niche or creating a false header, requires different types of openings. To install a niche, or for that matter a medicine cabinet or narrow shelving that fits between the wall studs, you must remove the drywall and attach the fixture to the adjacent studs.

If you are making a large opening, remove studs and install a header to carry the load imposed by the ceiling above it. Cut studs and install headers only on non-load-carrying walls. Leave alterations to load-carrying walls to the professionals.

False Headers. Use ladder framing to create false headers in openings between rooms that have a floor-to-ceiling pass-through. This is a common detail of center-hall homes, where wide openings to a dining room or living room reach all the way to the ceiling and don't really separate the rooms.

Solve the problem by building a 2×4 frame in the shape of a boxed-in ladder and installing it between the side walls. The frame has a full-length base and top plate, and short studs every 16 inches. It is wise to square up all the studs and nail them using 10d nails to keep the frame square. It's also helpful to use framing hardware.

Making a False Header

WHAT YOU'LL NEED

- Measuring tape and pencil
- Framing square
- 2x4 lumber and corner brackets
- Hammer and 10d common nails
- Drill-driver and 1⅝" drywall screws
- Drywall, joint compound, and tape
- Drywall knives

1 Measure the opening between the side walls; cut 2x4s for the bottom and top plates of the ladder frame.

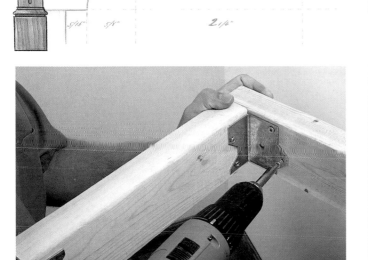

2 Square up the ladder with a framing square, and fasten hardware brackets in the corners with screws.

3 Cut short lengths of 2x4, and nail them 16 in. on center between the horizontal sections of the frame.

4 Set the ladder frame on temporary blocks, and fasten it to the ceiling joists and adjacent studs with screws.

5 Screw ½-in. drywall to the frame; add corner guards to the lower edges; and finish with tape and compound.

WHERE'S THE FRAMING?

When looking for studs or ceiling joists to nail or screw into, it helps to think about how the structures are framed. Ceiling joists, or floor joists from the floor above, rest on load-bearing walls and are typically spaced 16 inches on-center, meaning the distance from the center of one joist to the center of the next joist is 16 inches. In regular square or rectangular rooms, the joists always run parallel with two walls and perpendicular to the other two walls.

Wall Framing. Along solid wall planes, studs follow a 16 inch on-center layout. Door frames have doubled studs at either side and a header at the top of the opening. The header may be built-up, providing a wide area for nailing or may be a 2×4 laid flat above the door. Windows have a similar framing configuration. Plates at the top and bottom of a wall provide backing for ceiling and baseboard trim, respectively. Double top plates indicate that the wall is load-bearing; a single top plate usually indicates a non-load-bearing wall. Electrical outlets in walls typically have a stud at one side or the other, giving you a good place to start your search.

Finding Studs and Joists. The easiest way to locate studs and joists is with a stud sensor—an inexpensive electronic device that uses radio waves to sense density

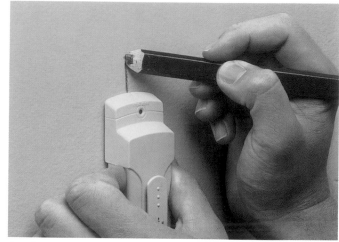

Stud sensors simplify framing searches. Follow the manufacturer's operating instructions for best results.

changes in walls and ceilings (see above). To use a stud sensor, move the device slowly over the wall or ceiling surface. A light will indicate when the sensor passes the edge of a stud, and it stays on until the sensor reaches the opposite edge. Mark both edges of the stud or joist; then measure from the center to find other framing members. You can also locate framing the old-fashioned way: tap the wall or ceiling surface lightly with a hammer, gradually moving sideways until you hear the tone of the tapping change pitch. Mark the area; then drive a finish nail through the surface material to verify the stud or joist location.

When using the stud sensor and/or nail method, there are a few things that can throw you off track. Old plaster walls and ceilings have a layer of wood lath between the

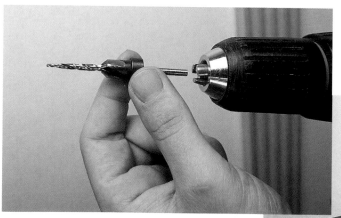

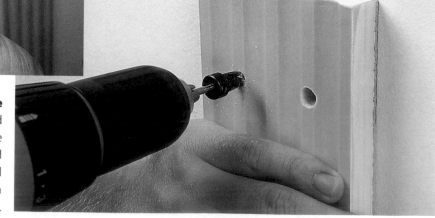

A combination countersink/counterbore bit is a great tool for screwing shelving and trimwork to walls, above. The hole on the right will accept a screw that will be recessed below the surface. The hole can then be filled with putty or a wood plug. When working on hollow walls, use hollow-wall anchors.

framing and the plaster surface. The lath framework can provide some support but should not be relied upon for heavy items. When nailed into, lath will feel spongy compared with the solid resistance of a stud or joist. Some stud sensors have a "deep scan" setting which helps locate framing through layers of plaster and lath. Also, while standard framing is 16 inches on center, some walls and many ceilings are framed with 24-inch-on-center spacing. And don't be surprised to find framing that's an inch or more off layout. (Upon making such a discovery, it's customary to curse your home's builder.)

USING HOLLOW-WALL ANCHORS

Hollow-wall anchors secure molding and other material to walls and ceilings where no framing or backing is present. If you haven't bought anchors in a while, you might be surprised by the range of styles available. One of the best versions is a screw-type drywall anchor with a self-piloting tip and coarse threads that hold tightly to the crumbly material. Some anchors are made specifically for plaster walls.

Use hollow-wall anchors designed to hold the weight of the object when installing shelving without stud backing.

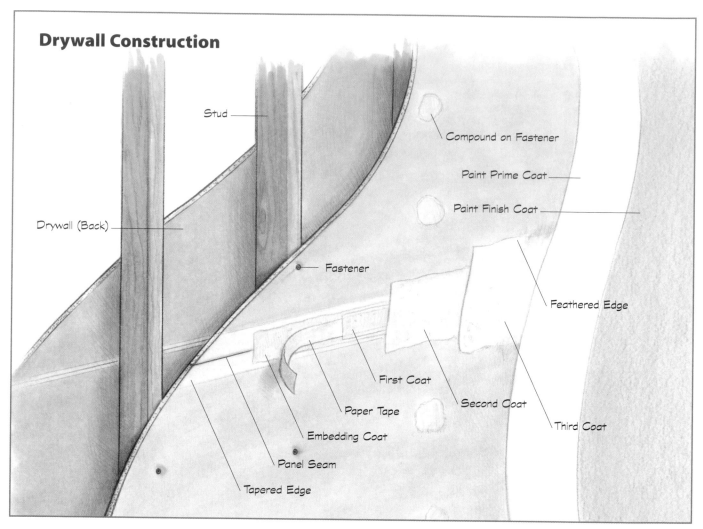

Drywall Construction

Stud

Compound on Fastener

Paint Prime Coat

Paint Finish Coat

Drywall (Back)

Fastener

Feathered Edge

First Coat

Second Coat

Paper Tape

Third Coat

Embedding Coat

Panel Seam

Tapered Edge

INSTALLING & FINISHING DRYWALL

A complete drywall project requires some inexpensive hand tools and a power drill-driver or drywall screwgun (available at rental centers). For a regular drill, you might want to buy a clutch-driver that stops turning the screw at the proper depth (as a screwgun does). The hand tools include a utility knife and straightedge, a mud pan (for holding compound), a 6- and a 10- or 12-inch drywall knife, and a 150-grit sanding sponge. For most applications, ½-inch drywall is best, unless you're matching old drywall of a different thickness. Use coarse-thread drywall screws for wood framing or fine-thread (Type S) drywall screws for steel framing.

Try to minimize the seams when planning a drywall layout. There is a slight taper along the long edge of the drywall sheets, so taping is less conspicuous. There is no taper along the short edge.

SMART TIP | Cutting Curves

The easiest way to cut drywall to fit around a curved opening is to screw a sheet of drywall in place and use a drywall saw to cut around the opening. The framing of the curve will act as a guide for your saw.

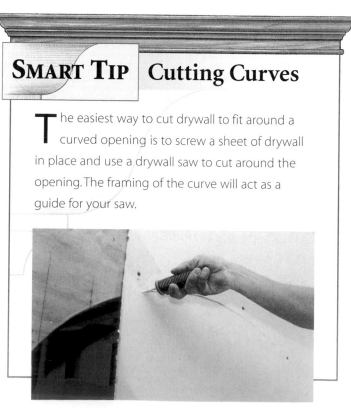

Installing Drywall

WHAT YOU'LL NEED

◆ Measuring tape, pencil, and utility knife
◆ Hammer and drywall nails
◆ Drill-driver and drywall screws
◆ Caulking gun and construction adhesive
◆ 4' T-square, panel lifter, and drywall
◆ 6" and 10" or 12" taping knives
◆ Joint compound, tape, and mud pan
◆ Corner bead
◆ 150-grit sandpaper and sanding pole
◆ Safety glasses

1 Cut through the drywall's face paper, using a utility knife and straightedge. Snap the waste piece back to break the gypsum core; then cut through the back paper.

2 Attach the drywall to the framing using screws. Each screw should dimple the face paper slightly without breaking through. Fasten every 8 in. along the edges and every 12 in. in the field of the panel.

3 To tape seams, spread a thin layer of compound using a 6-in. knife, then lay paper joint tape into the compound. Smooth the tape with a clean knife, making sure the tape is fully adhered and flat.

4 Fold tape in half along the crease to finish inside corners (top). Install corner bead at outside corners, and finish by running the knife along the beaded edge (bottom).

5 Apply two finishing coats using a 10- or 12-in. knife, sanding between coats to remove imperfections. Cover the screw dimples with three coats of compound. Final-sand all compound smooth.

RESOURCE GUIDE

The following list of manufacturers and associations is meant to be a general guide to additional industry and product-related sources. It is not intended as a listing of products and manufacturers represented by the photographs in this book.

PUBLICATIONS

Books

The Elements of Style: A Practical Encyclopedia of Interior Architectural Details from 1485 to the Present
Stephen Calloway, General Editor
Elizabeth Cromley, Consultant Editor
New York: Simon & Schuster, 1991, 1996

Period Details
Martin and Judith Miller
New York: Crown Publishers, Inc., 1987

More Period Details
Judith Miller
New York: Clarkson N. Potter Publishers, 1999

Periodicals

Old House Journal and *Old House Journal Restoration Directory*
Good information and advice offered both on-line and in print.
Subscriptions: 800-234-3797
www.oldhousejournal.com

Old House Interiors
Web site is a good resource for finding and researching vendors.
Subscriptions: 800-462-0211
www.oldhouseinteriors.com

Preservation magazine
National Trust for Historic Preservation
1785 Massachusetts Ave., NW
Washington, DC 20036
202-588-6000
www.nationaltrust.org

GENERAL RESOURCES

Information on historic architecture and the use of historically accurate architectural details and decorating.

The Society for the Preservation of New England Antiquities
141 Cambridge St.
Boston, MA 02114
617-227-3956
www.spnea.org

National Trust for Historic Preservation
1785 Massachusetts Ave., NW
Washington, D.C. 20036
202-588-6000
www.nationaltrust.org

PRODUCTS

Architectural Products by Outwater, LLC
Products include natural and synthetic moldings, flexible trim, niches, shutters, columns, ceiling medallions, tin ceiling tiles, and prefabricated arches.
4 Passaic St.
Wood-Ridge, NJ 07075
800 835-4400
www.outwater.com

Arcways
Manufacturer of metal and wood staircases and stair parts, including balusters, newels, fittings, inlaid tread borders, and starting steps.
P.O. Box 763
Neenah, WI 54957
800-558-5096
www.arcways.com

BuyPlantationShutters.com
Supplier of natural and synthetic shutters, shutter hardware, and blinds, with good information for the do-it-yourselfer.
102 Aubrey Dr.
Butler, PA 16001
800-316-9468
www.buyplantationshutters.com

CAS Design Center
Products include natural and synthetic moldings, columns and pilasters, niches, ceiling domes, and medallions.
12201 Currency Circle
Forney, TX 75126
800 662-1221
www.casdesign.com

Chadsworth's 1-800-Columns
Products include natural and synthetic columns and pillars.
277 North Front St.
Wilmington, NC 28401
800-486-2118
www.columns.com

Classic Details
Supplier of natural and synthetic moldings, niches, ceiling medallions and domes, stair brackets, carved ornaments, and more.
Southern Rose
P.O. Box 280144
Columbia, SC 29228
www.classicdetails.com

Cumberland Woodcraft Co., Inc.
Products include natural and synthetic moldings, fireplace mantels and mantel surround kits, brackets, and ceiling medallions.
P.O. Drawer 609
Carlisle, PA 17013
800-367-1884
www.cumberlandwoodcraft.com

CurveMakers Inc.
Supplier of kits to convert standard wall openings into arched openings.
612 W. Hargett St.
Raleigh, NC 27603
919-821-5792
www.curvemakers.com

Decorative Concepts
Products include fireplace mantels, mantel surround kits.
11880 West President Dr., Suite F
Boise, ID 83713
866-328-8033
www.decorativeconcepts.net

The Decorators Supply Corporation
Products include plaster and wood moldings, fireplace mantels, niche shells, and ornamental inlays.
3610 S. Morgan St.
Chicago, IL 60609
773-847-6300
www.decoratorssupply.com

Elegance in Wood
Maker of wood window cornices, decorative brackets, and wall shelves.
8258 Maple Rd.
Akron, NY 14001
716-542-7095
www.eleganceinwood.com

Kestrel Shutters
Products include raised panel, louvered and cutout shutters, decorative paneled shutters and folding screens, fabric shutters, and shutter hardware.
9 East Race St.
Stowe, PA 19464
800-494-4321
www.diyshutters.com

The Mantel Shop, Inc.
Products include fireplace mantels, mantel surround kits.
730 W. Paseo Verde Dr., Unit A
Nogales, AZ 85621
888-367-5771
www.mantelshop.com

Maple Grove Restorations
Products include custom-made raised-panel shutters and wall treatments, wainscoting, fireplace mantels, and surrounds.
Andover, CT
860-742-5432
www.maple-grove.com

M-Boss Inc.
Supplier of metal ceiling panels and accessories.
5350 Grant Ave.
Cleveland, OH 44125
866-886-2677
www.mbossinc.com

Zoroufy Stair Rods
Products include stair rods and stair holds.
Madison, WI
608-833-9026
www.zoroufy.com

ARCHITECTURAL SALVAGE

Old House Journal Restoration Directory
www.oldhousejournal.com
800-234-3797

PreservationWeb
Web and print source for regional restoration products
and services.
P.O. Box 1329
Vienna, VA 22180
800-707-4330
www.preservationweb.com

SalvageWeb
Website provides salvage book recommendations and
regional salvage supplier information.
www.salvageweb.com

**Salvo: Architectural Salvage, Garden Antiques &
Reclaimed Building Materials**
Extensive Web resources and publisher of several print
publications.
P.O. Box 333
Cornhill on Tweed
TD 12 4YJ, Northumberland, England
Telephone: +44 1890 820333
www.salvoweb.com

Old World Stoneworks
Manufacturer of cast stone mantels and overmantels.
5400 Miller Ave.
Dallas, TX 75206
800-600-8336
www.oldstoneworks.com

Smith+Noble
Supplier of window treatments, including wood and fabric
cornices and shutters.
800-560-0027
www.smithandnoble.com

Style Solutions, Inc.
Products include synthetic decorative trim, moldings,
niches, and medallions.
960 West Barre Rd.
Archbold, OH 43502
800-446-3040
www.stylesolutionsinc.com

Westfire Manufacturing, Inc.
Supplier of stair parts, including newel posts, balusters,
and handrails.
8751 SW Pamlico Ct.
Tualatin, OR 97062
800-692-6996
www.westfiremfg.com

W.F. Norman Corporation
Manufacturer of decorative metal ceilings, including panels,
cornices, and moldings.
214 N. Cedar
P.O. Box 323
Nevada, MO 64772
800-641-4038
www.wfnorman.com

GLOSSARY

Alkyd-based A paint containing synthetic resins. Cleans up with paint thinner or other toxic solvents. Often referred to as oil-based.

Analogous colors Adjacent colors on the color wheel that share an underlying hue.

Backsaw A straight fine-toothed saw often used with a miter box to create clean-edged miter cuts for trim and picture frames.

Baseboard A trim board attached as part of a base treatment to the bottom of a wall where it meets the floor.

Bead A general term referring to a convex, semicircular profile on a molding.

Bench plane A large tool (compared with a block plane) designed to shave wood off the surface of a board.

Bevel An angle other than 90 degrees cut into the thickness of a piece of lumber or other material.

Blocking Small pieces of lumber used to fill a gap in framing or provide a nailing surface (sometimes called a nailer). For example, triangular blocking might be used to bridge the gap between the wall and the ceiling and provide a nailing surface for angled crown molding.

Block plane A small single-handled tool that shaves wood from boards.

Building code Printed set of design and material specifications governing construction in a given municipality or geographical area. Local or municipal building codes supersede all other codes, such as regional or national codes.

Casing The general term for any trim that surrounds a door or window.

Caulk A variety of flexible materials used to fill seams and seal connections. The caulk used to fill seams around trim is usually made of siliconized acrylic.

Chair rail A horizontal band of trim installed on a wall between the floor and the ceiling. Usually placed 30 to 36 inches above the floor.

Chalk line A marking tool consisting of a string wound inside a container filled with colored chalk that you use to mark long straight lines.

Chamfer A bevel resulting from cutting the corner off of the edge of a board, typically at a 45-degree angle.

Color wheel A graphic representation of the full color spectrum used to describe and compare the relationship among different paint colors.

Column A vertical support member, typically with a cylindrical or square shaft. Also called a pillar. Classical column designs include a base, shaft, and capital.

Combing A decorative paint technique in which you remove a certain amount of paint by dragging a comb or similar object across the wet surface.

Compound miter saw A power saw mounted on a pivoting arm and a swiveling base that allows you to make both bevel and miter cuts.

Cope To cut the end of a molding so that its profile will match that of an abutting piece of similar molding.

Coping saw A small handsaw with a thin, flexible blade used for cutting tight curves.

Corbel A carved block or bracket projecting from a wall to support a beam or other horizontal member. Also called a bracket.

Corner bead Metal or plastic angle trim used for finishing and protecting the corners of drywalled surfaces.

Cornice Any molding (typically large) or group of moldings used in the corner between a wall and a ceiling.

Countersink To drive a fastener below the surface of a board in order to give the surface a more finished appearance. Also, the name given to the drill bit used to cut a recess in a board in order to make it possible to sink a screwhead below the board's surface.

Cove A general term referring to a concave semicircular profile on a molding.

Crosscut A cut across the grain of a piece of lumber. A general-purpose crosscut saw has a blade designed for this purpose with about eight teeth per inch.

Crown molding Single-piece molding that installs at an angle to it's adjoining surfaces. Typically used to adorn the intersection between a wall and ceiling.

Dado A wide flat-bottomed groove cut at a right angle to the grain of a piece of wood. Also, the lower area of a wall (below a chair rail) that is wallpapered.

Dead-ending The treatment of a piece of molding at its end; usually a chamfer or a return.

Dentil molding A molding with a pattern of alternating blocks and spaces.

Door casing The trim applied to a wall around the edge of a door frame.

Drywall A sheet material made of gypsum and paper used to cover the interior walls of most homes.

Egg-and-dart molding A molding pattern that includes egg-shaped relief carvings.

Entablature In classical architecture, the horizontal assembly supported by columns or other structure and consisting of an architrave, frieze, and cornice.

File A long thin metal tool with a rough surface used to shape material. Often, the term file is reserved for fine-surfaced tools used on metal, and the term rasp is reserved for coarse-surfaced tools used on wood.

Finger joint A joint used to make long lengths of material from shorter lengths. The ends of the short lengths are cut in a fingerlike interlocking pattern and glued together. Less expensive moldings are often made by finger joining short pieces of lumber together.

Framing The structural skeleton, typically wood, of a house.

Frieze The middle, relatively flat, section of an entablature. Also the wall area between a picture rail or frieze molding and the ceiling or cornice molding.

Hardwood Generally, the wood of large deciduous trees such as maple, oak, and poplar.

Header Horizontal supporting member, such as a beam or lintel, spanning the top of a wall opening. Also the decorative trim assembly over an opening.

Human scale Architectural term describing proportions well suited to the human body. Also a design concept aimed at appealing to a human's sense of comfort and shelter in a living space.

Inside corner A corner in which two surfaces, such as walls, meet at an angle less than 180 degrees.

Jamb One piece of the frame around a window or door.

Joint compound A soupy material made primarily of crushed limestone and liquid vinyl used to repair holes and fill joints between panels of gypsum drywall.

Joists Horizontal framing members of a floor or ceiling frame.

Kerf The material a saw blade removes in a single cut, usually about ⅛ of an inch, or the thickness of the blade.

Latex-based Paints that can be thinned and cleaned up with water.

Level Term used to define a surface or line that is perfectly horizontal. Also, the name given to a variety of instruments used to determine whether a surface or line is perfectly horizontal.

Masking Covering a surface when painting near it, usually with masking tape.

Medallion A decorative, usually round relief carving applied to a wall or ceiling.

Miter An angle cut into the face or thickness of a piece of lumber or other material to form a miter joint.

Miter box A wood, plastic, or metal jig fitted with a handsaw, designed for cutting wood at various angles.

Molding Decorative strips of wood or plastic used in various kinds of trimwork.

Monochromatic scheme A paint scheme in which the trim, walls, and ceilings in a room are all painted the same color but with different values.

Nail set A blunt-pointed metal tool used to sink nailheads below the surface of wood. The pointed end is held on the nailhead as the other end is struck with a hammer.

Outside corner A corner in which the faces of the walls project out and away from each other in an angle greater than 180 degrees.

Palladian Architectural style inspired by the classical designs of Italian Renaissance architect Andrea Palladio (1508–1580).

Pedestal An extended rectangular or square base of a column.

Pediment A triangular decorative feature usually spanning above an opening such as a door, window, or fireplace, or placed above a series of columns.

Pilaster A shallow, square-edged column projecting from a wall or other vertical surface. Typically, a decorative treatment made to appear as a supporting element.

Plate joiner A power tool that cuts slots in the edges of boards so that they can be joined by inserting and gluing a wooden wafer (biscuit) in the slots; also called a biscuit joiner.

Plinth A rectangular block serving as the base of vertical door casing or a pilaster.

Plumb An expression describing a perfectly vertical surface or line. A plumb surface will meet a level surface at 90 degrees to form a right angle.

Plates The horizontal members secured to the ends of the studs at the top and bottom of a wall frame.

Power miter saw A circular saw mounted on a pivoting base with angle measurements that is used to cut accurate angle cuts in lumber and other materials.

Predrill To drill a hole in a piece of lumber before nailing or screwing it to a surface to make driving the fastener easier and to prevent the lumber from splitting.

Rabbet A notch cut into the edge of a piece of lumber, generally so that another piece of lumber can be set into the notch to join the two pieces at a right angle.

Ragging A decorative paint technique that involves adding or removing layers of paint using a rag.

Rail Horizontal trimwork installed on a wall between the cornice and base trim. Also, the horizontal members of the framework of such systems as doors, sashes, and cabinets.

Rafters The principal supporting members of a roof frame, spanning between the walls and the roof peak.

Rasp A long thin metal tool with a rough-toothed surface used to shape wood.

Return A small piece of molding attached to the end of a long run of molding to carry the profile from the front of the molding back to the wall.

Rip A cut made in the direction of the grain on a piece of lumber. A ripsaw is designed for this type of cutting and has a blade with about six teeth per inch.

Roundover bit A router bit used to cut a semicircular profile along the edge of a board.

Router A power tool with a rotating shaft that accepts a variety of specially shaped bits. Designed for many purposes, such as cutting contours on the edges of molding or grooves into the face of a piece of lumber.

Sandpaper Sandy grit on a paper backing used to smooth wood and other materials. Numbers printed on the backing refer to grit size. Higher numbers indicate finer grits, while lower numbers indicate coarser grits that remove more material.

Scarf joint The connection between two pieces of trim joined by overlapping opposing miters in order to disguise the joint.

Sliding T-bevel An adjustable tool, often called a bevel square or bevel gauge, used to capture and transfer angles.

Softwood Generally, the wood of coniferous, needle-bearing trees such as pine, fir, or spruce.

Soffit A framed and finished structure that projects down from a ceiling. Also the material used to cover the underside of roof eaves.

Sponging Adding or removing layers of paint for decorative effect using a sponge.

Stile The outer vertical members of the framework found on doors, sashes, cabinets, and wainscot systems.

Studs The vertical members of a wall frame. In residential construction, studs typically are spaced at 16- or 24-inch intervals.

Toenailing Attaching the end of a board to the face of another by nailing at a steep angle.

Tripartite A decorative wall treatment consisting of three horizontal sections bordered by baseboard, chair rail, and picture rail (or frieze), and cornice molding.

Wainscoting Any trim or decorative finish along the lower portion of a wall.

Window casing Trim that surrounds the edges of a window frame.

Window stool The horizontal surface installed below the sash of a window, often called a windowsill.

Wood filler A puttylike material used to fill nailholes and other imperfections in the surface of wood.

PHOTO & DESIGNER CREDITS

All photography by Jessie Walker Associates, unless otherwise noted.

page 8: designer: Steve Guerrant **page 10:** *top* designer: Anthony Constanza; *bottom right and bottom left* architect: Stephen R. Knutson **page 11:** *top* designer: Amy Sandack, Drury Design **page 14:** architect: Paul Janicki **page 15:** architect: Julie Rearick **page 16:** designer: Diane Wendall **page 18:** architect: Paul Janicki **page 20:** designer: Glen Meidbreder Bath Designs **page 21:** *bottom* designer: Alan Portnoy **page 24:** design team: Jim & Jean Wagner **page 25:** designer: Chris Garrett **page 27:** *bottom* designer: David T. Smith **page 36:** *top* designer: Carol Knott, ASID **page 38:** *center* designer: M.J. May Building Restoration; *bottom* architect: Stephen R. Knutson **page 45:** architect: Stephen R. Knutson **pages 48–49:** *center* designer: Greene & Proppe Designs; *bottom right* architect: Stephen R. Knutson; *bottom left* designer: Jane Irvine **page 50:** designer: Gail Plechaty **page 51:** designer: Daniel DuBay **page 53:** *top* designer: Kim Elias; *bottom* designer: Suzanne Murphy **page 57:** *bottom* designer Mastro & Skylar **page 59:** designer: Shea Lubeke **page 63:** designer: Nancy & Ed Hillner **page 65:** designer: Eva Stefanski **page 72:** designer: Jeanne Goss **page 77:** *bottom* designer: Dave McFadden/Past Basket Cabinetry **page 78:** *bottom* architect: Linda Searle **page 80:** *top* architect: Stephen R. Knutson; *bottom* designer: Michael Muha **page 81:** architect: Stephen R. Knutson **page 84:** *top* designer: Cheryl Janz & Georgean Pragit, ASID & Jackie Bruggenthies, Allied ASID/ Marshall Fields' Design Studio **page 88:** designer: Marsha Jones **page 93:** *bottom right* designer: Chris Garrett **page 94:** *top* designer: Jane Hopper, ASID **page 96:** designer: Jane Irvine **page 101:** *top* architect: David Raino **page 106:** designer: Joy Prisching **page 109:** designer: Sevvonco Custom Home Builders **page 112:** *top* designer: Daniel DuBay **page 113:** *top* designer: Anita Phillipsborn **page 116:** *bottom* designer: David T. Smith **page 117:** *top* designer: Elinor Gordon, ASID **page 122:** *bottom* designer: David T. Smith **page 126:** designer: Richard Abrahmson **page 128:** designer: Mastro & Skylar **page 129:** architect: Stephen R. Knutson **page 130:** *bottom* designer: Jane Hopper, ASID **page 135:** designer: Jane Hopper, ASID **page 137:** *top* designer: Liz Kavanaugh; *bottom* designer: Cornerstone Builders **page 140:** *top* designer: Daniel DuBay **page 144:** designer: Richard Abrahmson **page 146:** *top* designer: Alice Wisegarver **page 147:** *top* designer: Jane Levy Designs **page 149:** *top* architect: George Larson; *bottom* designer: Sevvonco Custom Home Builders **page 151:** *top* designer: Sevvonco Custom Home Builders **page 153:** designer: Jean Stoffer **page 154:** designer: Adele Lampert **page 157:** architect: Paul Janicki **page 159:** architect: Stephen R. Knutson **page 160:** designer: Joe Walters **page 161:** designer: Meidbreder Building Group **page 162:** owners: Bob & Lorel McMillan **page 165:** architect: David Poulton, designer: Kelly Hutchinson **page 166:** architects: McBride & Kelly Architects **page 168:** architect: Dave McFadden **page 169:** *top* architect/designer: Dave McFadden **page 170:** owners: Bob & Lorel McMillan **page 173:** *top* architect: David Frankel; *center* architect: Jim Tharp **page 174:** designer: Jane Levy Designs **page 176:** *top* owners: Bob & Lorel McMillan **page 178:** architect: Gary Frank **page 184:** *bottom* designer: Alice Allen **page 185:** designer: Paul Munro **page 186:** designer: Mary DeBuhr **page 189:** *top* designer: Joan Babb **pages 190–191:** *center* designer: Lana Thorstensen; *bottom right* designer: Stephen R. Knutson **page 196:** photographer: Gary David Gold/CH **page 199:** *top* photographer: John Parsekian/CH; *bottom* photographer Gary David Gold/CH **page 200:** Brian C. Nieves/CH **page 201:** architect: Thomas Swarthout **page 202:** designer: McCauley Designs **page 203:** *top* photography Gary David Gold/CH **pages 204–205:** *left and top row* photographer John Parsekian/CH; *bottom* architect: Stephen R. Knotson **pages 206–208:** photographer: John Parsekian/CH **pages 210–211:** photographer: John Parsekian/CH

SOURCES

Photographers: Jessie Walker, Glencoe, IL; 847-835-0522. John Parsekian, Bloomfield, NJ; 973-748-9717. Gary David Gold, Albany, NY; 518-434-4887

Designers, Architects & Builders: Richard Abrahmson, Designer/RJA Designs, Geneva, IL. Jackie Bruggenthies, Designer, Allied ASID, Oak Brook, IL. Elinor Gordon, Designer, ASID, Chicago, IL. Steve Guerrant, Designer, Chicago, IL. Jane Hopper, ASID, Winnetka, IL. Jane Irvine, Designer, Kildeer, IL. Paul Janicki, Architect, Chicago, IL. Stephen R. Knutson, Architect, Chicago, IL. Cheryl Janz, Designer, ASID, Oak Brook. IL. Marshall Fields' Design Studio, Oak Brook, IL. Mastro/Skylar, Designers, Chicago, IL. Dave McFadden/Past Basket Cabinetry, Geneva, IL. Lorel & Robert McMillan, Glencoe, IL. Michael Muha, Designer, Birmingham, MI. Gail Plechaty, Designer, Old Mill Creek, IL. Alan Portnoy, Designer, Chicago, IL. David Poulton, Architect, Chicago, IL. Georgean Pragit, Designer, ASID, Oak Brook, IL. Amy Sandack/Drury Designs, Glenn Ellyn, IL. Linda Searle, Architect, Chicago, IL. Sevvonco Custom Home Builders, Palatine, IL. David T. Smith, Designer, Morrow, OH. Jean Stoffer, Designer, River Forest. IL.

INDEX

Have a home improvement, decorating, or gardening project? Look for these and other fine **Creative Homeowner books** wherever books are sold.

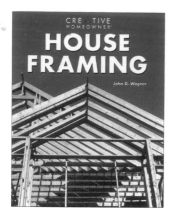

Designed to walk you through the framing basics. Over 400 illustrations. 208 pp.; 8¹/₂"×10⁷/₈"
BOOK#: 277655

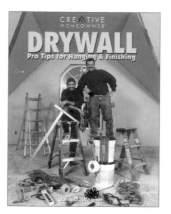

A complete guide covering all aspects of drywall. Over 250 color illustrations. 144 pp.; 8¹/₂"×10⁷/₈"
BOOK #: 278315

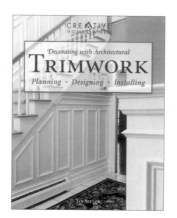

Transform a room with trimwork. Over 450 color photos and illustrations. 208 pp.; 8¹/₂"×10⁷/₈"
BOOK #: 277495

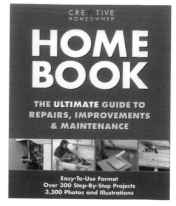

The ultimate home improvement reference manual. Over 300 step-by-step projects. 608 pp.; 9"×10⁷/₈"
BOOK#: 267855

Complete DIY tile instruction. Over 350 color photos and illustrations. 160 pp.; 8¹/₂"×10⁷/₈"
BOOK#: 277524

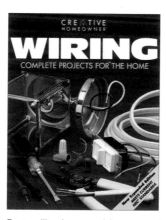

Best-selling house-wiring manual. Over 850 color photos and illustrations. 288 pp.; 8¹/₂"×10⁷/₈"
BOOK#: 278237

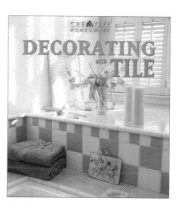

Explores the many design possibilities of tile, including advice for indoor and outdoor projects. Over 250 color photos. 176 pp.; 9"×10"
BOOK#: 279824

Learn how to make the most of color. Ideas for selecting and coordinating color schemes. More than 200 color photos. 176 pp.; 9"×10"
BOOK#: 287264

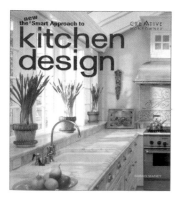

Newly revised, has all the answers for a new kitchen. Over 260 color photographs. 208 pp.; 9"×10"
BOOK #: 279946

How to work with space, color, pattern, and texture. Over 400 photos. 288 pp.; 9"×10"
BOOK #: 279672

An impressive guide to garden design and plant selection. More than 800 photos. 320 pp.; 9"×10"
BOOK #: 274615

For the beginning and experienced gardener. Over 500 color photos and illustrations. 208 pp.; 9"×10"
BOOK #: 274032

For more information, and to order direct, call 800-631-7795; in New Jersey 201-934-7100.
Please visit our Web site at www.creativehomeowner.com